How to
Expand, Modernise
PCs and Compatibles

D0351281

Other Titles of Interest

How to
Expand, Modernise and Repair
PCs and Compatibles

by
R. A. Penfold

BERNARD BABANI (publishing) LTD
THE GRAMPIANS
SHEPHERDS BUSH ROAD
LONDON W6 7NF
ENGLAND

Please Note

Although every care has been taken with the production of this book to ensure that any projects, designs, modifications and/or programs etc. contained herewith, operate in a correct and safe manner and also that any components specified are normally available in Great Britain, the Publishers and Author do not accept responsibility in any way for the failure, including fault in design, of any project, design, modification or program to work correctly or to cause damage to any other equipment that it may be connected to or used in conjunction with, or in respect of any other damage or injury that may be so caused, nor do the Publishers accept responsibility in any way for the failure to obtain specified components.

Notice is also given that if equipment that is still under warranty is modified in any way or used or connected with home-built equipment then that warranty may be void.

© 1990 BERNARD BABANI (publishing) LTD

First Published — April 1990
Reprinted — August 1991
Reprinted — December 1992
Revised Edition — January 1994

British Library Cataloguing in Publication Data:
Penfold, R. A.
    How to expand, modernise and repair PCs and compatibles
    1. Microcomputers. Maintenance & repair
    I. Title
    621.3916

    ISBN 0 85934 216 6

Printed and Bound in Great Britain by Cox & Wyman Ltd, Reading.

Preface

Since its introduction in 1981 the IBM PC has undergone continuous changes and developments. In general, IBM themselves have led the way, but in recent times the various "clone" manufacturers have introduced some innovations of their own. Despite all the improvements that have been made, and the increased capabilities of modern PCs, a PC still remains very much a PC. Software and add-ons for the original machines will still function perfectly well in a modern PC. A factor that has certainly aided the popularity of PCs and compatibles is their open architecture. IBM published the full specification of the PC expansion slots, making it easy for third party suppliers to produce and sell PC expansion cards of various types. This has led to numerous specialist add-ons for the PC being produced, as well as a good range of mainstream products.

While expanding a PC is, in the main, a reasonably straightforward affair, there are inevitably some complications to most aspects of PC upgrading. The main purpose of this book is to first explain the basics of PC hardware, and to then help untangle the difficulties that can arise when undertaking the more popular of PC upgrades. The topics covered include floppy and hard disk drives, memory expansion, display adaptors and monitors, maths co-processors, ports, and keyboards.

Many PC users prefer, as far as possible, to do their own maintenance and this subject is covered in Chapter 5. Assembling your own PC might seem to be a rather ambitious task, but the modular construction of these computers means that it is in fact much easier than one might expect to put together a PC to exactly meet your desired specification. With all the necessary parts for a PC now being readily available, this is an increasingly popular way of obtaining a PC, and one that is described in the penultimate chapter of this book. The final chapter covers developments to-date since the book was first written.

R. A. Penfold

Warning

Note that in the U.K. certain upgrades might invalidate the manufacturer's warranty (especially upgrades that involve adding something other than an expansion card to the computer). However, provided you do not damage anything when upgrading a computer, the retailer's guarantee is probably still valid. As manufacturer's guarantees often go beyond the statutory minimum requirements of a retailer's warranty, you might still be losing out to some degree. The law governing guarantees might be different to this in other countries. If a computer has some form of on-site or other maintenance agreement, this might also be affected by upgrades. It is advisable to read the "small print" in the agreement before proceeding with any upgrade. If you are in any doubt it is best to first check with the retailer and/or manufacturer.

Trademarks

Contents

Chapter 1

PC OVERVIEW

There are many possible reasons for the unrivalled popularity of the IBM PCs and the numerous compatible machines, which have been the standard business microcomputer for several years now. One contributory factor is certainly their enormous expansion potential. The basic computer, or "system unit" as it is generally called, is unusable on its own. It requires the addition of disk drives, a monitor, a keyboard, and even such things as an add-in disk controller and a display generator before it will provide any useful function. This modular approach without even such things as the display generator and disk controller on the main circuit board has been the cause of a certain amount of criticism, but in truth it is a very good way of doing things.

If all you require is a very basic computer with a single disk drive and a monochrome display, then you can buy a PC compatible of that type. You do not need to spend money on expensive disk drives or colour monitors that you do not need or want. If, on the other hand, you are interested in graphics applications and require high resolution multi-colour graphics plus a large and fast hard disk drive, you will have a choice of several PC compatible systems that offer a suitable specification. With requirements for computer systems that fall somewhere between these two extremes you are likely to be spoiled for choice, with a vast number of suitable systems to choose from. If you can not find something that exactly meets your requirements, then it is possible to buy a basic computer system and add in suitable peripherals yourself. Due to IBM's so-called "open architecture" policy (publishing full technical details of their microcomputers so that third party manufacturers can produce add-ons for them), the range of add-on boards and other peripherals for the PC series runs into many hundreds.

1

In this book we will mainly be concerned with the hardware side of PC compatible computing. In this first chapter we will take a look at PC hardware in general, going into any great detail on some subjects, but considering others in a superficial manner. Subsequent chapters provide detailed information on several topics not fully discussed in this chapter (disk drives, display cards, etc.). Those who are already familiar with the general principles of PC hardware and expansion will probably be familiar with some of the topics covered. Readers in this category might like to skip over some sections of this chapter. Those who are not familiar with PC hardware should study this chapter in some detail before progressing to any of the other chapters that cover a topic of particular interest to them. Trying to expand a PC without understanding the differences between the various types of PC and their general make up could easily lead to some costly mistakes.

Software Compatibility
The term "software compatibility" in a PC context generally refers to the ability (or lack of it) to run standard IBM PC software designed to operate under either the PC/DOS or MS/DOS operating systems. These two operating systems can for virtually all practical purposes be regarded as interchangeable. PC/DOS is the operating system produced by Microsoft for use with real IBM PCs, whereas MS/DOS is the version for compatibles. In theory, any software written to run under PC/MS/DOS should run on any computer that has either of these operating systems up and running properly. In practice there is a complication in that much software sometimes controls the computer's hardware by reading from it and writing to it directly, rather than going through the operating system.

The problem here is that any variations in the hardware are supposed to be handled by the operating system. If data is written to a printer port, the operating system should ensure that the data is sent to the right piece of hardware, and that the flow of data to the printer is controlled properly. If data is sent direct to the hardware by the program, and it monitors the hardware directly to see if the printer is ready to receive data, there is a risk of incompatibility. In these circumstances the program will only run properly if the computer has the right peripheral components at the right places in the computer's input/output map. The operating system will not be involved in the exchange of data, and will not intervene to ensure that it all goes smoothly.

As quite a large number of programs rely on direct control of the hardware in order to achieve a suitably fast operating speed, it is important that PC compatibles accurately mimic the hardware of the computers they are trying to be compatible with. In reality simply running a computer under the MS/DOS operating system is not good enough. Probably all modern compatibles achieve good compatibility in this respect. I have used several IBM PC compatible machines in recent years, and do not recall ever experiencing any problems with software that would not run due to hardware incompatibilities of this type.

ROM BIOS

An important factor for good compatibility is the quality of the ROM BIOS. ROM stands for "read only memory", and it is a component (or two in the case of AT type computers) which contains a computer program. The program they contain is the BIOS, or "basic input/output system". The first function of the BIOS is to run a few diagnostic checks to ensure that the computer is up and running properly. It then looks on the disk drives in search of the operating system, which it then loads into the computer's memory. The operating system then takes over, but the BIOS contains software routines that can be utilized by the operating system.

You will often encounter the term "booting" or "booting-up", which refers to this process of the operating system being automatically loaded from disk and run. This term is derived from the fact that operating system appears to load itself from memory, which is akin to pulling one's self up by one's bootlaces. Of course, the operating system only appears to be loading and running itself. The truth of the matter is that routines in the ROM BIOS are carrying out this process.

The software in the BIOS, or "firmware" as programs in this form is often termed, must not be an exact copy of the IBM original due to copyright restrictions. Several companies produce BIOS chips which do the same thing as the IBM original but by a different means so that copyright problems are avoided. Obviously this gives rise to the possibility of incompatibilities, but any modern BIOS should be well tried and tested. Again, I have used several IBM compatibles in recent years, using BIOS chips from manufacturers including Phoenix, Award, and AMI, and have yet to encounter any incompatibility problems.

What probably represents the greatest potential incompatibility problem is the vast array of different add-ons and "standards" for the IBM PCs and compatibles. Tremendous versatility being possible with a computer of any specification within reason. The price that has to be paid for this is the fact that there is probably no program that is compatible with every possible computer configuration, apart perhaps from genuinely text only programs. Even with these you could be faced with a computer capable of handling a hundred plus characters per line with around fifty lines per screenful, only to find that none of your software can actually take advantage of any enhanced screen modes.

The much given advice of buy the software that suits your requirements first and then the buy hardware to suit it afterwards, remains as good as it ever was. It is as well to bear in mind that there is almost always a significant gap between new "improved" hardware arriving on the scene, and software being updated to take advantage of it. If the item of hardware in question fails to achieve a reasonable degree of popularity, then it is quite likely that little or no software will ever be modified to suit it, or provided with suitable driver routines.

If you are upgrading a computer with any remotely

specialised or unusual graphics board or whatever, make quite sure it will be able to function in the desired manner with the software you wish to use with it. Check very carefully that you are getting something that will fit the bill. Add-on boards for IBM compatibles are often supplied complete with software of some description, such as drivers to enable the unit to operate with popular programs. But is the software for your particular version of the program, or some earlier version perhaps? Where possible it is advisable to actually try out the add-on with your software before parting with any money. Not all the software supplied with expansion cards is fully debugged and fully operational! The only way to find out for sure is to adopt the "suck it and see" approach.

PC Versions

The PCs and compatibles have evolved over a period of several years, and the more up-market systems in use today have specifications that bear little resemblance to the original IBM PC which was launched in 1981. The original had just 64k of memory, a monochrome text only display, and included a cassette port. The IBM compatible I am using to produce the text and drawings for this book has a total of nearly 4 megabytes (4096k) of RAM, a colour graphics board that can handle up to 800 by 600 pixels with 256 colours on-screen at once, plus two floppy disk drives and a 43 megabyte fast hard disk. It also uses a microprocessor that renders it several times faster than the original PC. Despite this, it is still highly compatible with the original computer. It can almost certainly run any software that will run on the original version of the computer, and can take any expansion card that is compatible with the original machine.

The opposite is not true though, and there is much software and a lot of expansion cards that will work in my AT compatible computer, but are unusable with the original computer, and some more recent compatibles come to that. It is worth considering basic details of the various versions of the IBM PC range, not just out of

5

historical interest, but because you need to know how your particular machine fits into the overall scheme of things in order to know what peripherals are compatible with it, and which ones are not. In some cases there are different versions of a product for different versions of the PC, and you need to be careful to obtain the right one.

Original PCs

The "PC" in IBM PC merely stands for "personal computer". This is a possible cause of confusion since the IBM PCs and compatibles are often referred to simply as "PCs", but this is also a general term for any microcomputer which is primarily intended for business rather than home use. Anyway, in this book the term "PC" will only be used to refer to the IBM PC family of computers and the many compatible machines.

The original PC has relatively limited expansion potential. It has facilities for five full length expansion slots, but with a maximum of only 256k RAM on the main circuit board, (64k on the earliest PCs), and slots being required for disk controllers, serial and parallel ports, and the display card, this is not quite as good as it might at first appear. To ease the problem, several manufacturers produce multi-function cards which give such things as an extra 384k of memory plus serial and parallel ports all on one card. This is certainly helpful, and not just with the early PCs. If you wish to use a lot of peripherals with a PC there is always a risk that you will run out of expansion slots. Multi-function boards often offer a means of getting around this problem.

Probably the main problem when trying to expand an early PC is that of its power supply. This has a rating of 63.5 watts, which is low in comparison to the ratings of around 150 watts for the later versions. 63.5 watts is actually quite a hefty power supply for a microcmputer, but it nevertheless provides little more power than the basic system requires. Anything more than the addition of one or two low power cards will require the fitting of a more beefy power supply unit, which usually means a

150 watt type, as fitted to some later versions of the PC, and most PC compatibles. Another problem is that the ROM BIOS has undergone a few changes over the years, and expansion of an early PC will usually require an updated ROM BIOS chip to be fitted.

Upgrading an early PC is certainly possible, but it is not necessarily a worthwhile proposition. It could be quite expensive — too expensive to be cost effective in fact. This is something that has to be taken on a case by case basis, but where an upgrade is essential it would seem that many users these days opt for buying a new system. Spending a great deal of money upgrading any computer that is a number of years old and possibly nearing the end of its operating life would clearly be a decidedly risky course of action.

There have been several more recent versions of the PC, including the "Convertible", which is a laptop computer. In fact several versions of the Convertible were produced. The nature of this computer is such that it is largely non-standard as far as expansion is concerned. As by PC standards it did not sell in large numbers, it has been out of production for some years, and most IBM compatible laptop and luggable PCs are not what could really be considered clones of the Convertible, we will not consider this computer any further in this publication. Neither will we bother with the PC Junior. This was designed to be a home computer version of the PC, but it never really caught on. I think I am correct in stating that it was never released onto the U.K. market, but was sold in some countries outside the U.S.A.

PC XT Computers
IBM introduced the PC XT in 1983, and it is this model rather than the original PC that tends to be considered as the "standard" PC. The "XT" part of the name is an abbreviation for extended, incidentally. It is an improvement on the original design in a number of ways. One of the improvements is that ability to have up to 640k of socketed RAM on the main circuit board, or

"motherboard" as it is usually termed. The original PCs had all the RAM chips soldered directly to the board, making it difficult and expensive to replace a faulty chip. With the ability to have 640k of RAM on the motherboard, which is the maximum that the design of the computer permits, there is no need to take up an expansion slot with a memory board if you need the full complement of RAM.

The expansion slot problem was eased anyway, by the inclusion of no less than eight slots on the motherboard. Even with slots occupied by disk controllers, serial and parallel ports, and a display board, there would still typically be four or five slots left for more exotic peripherals. Two of the slots are only suitable for short expansion boards. This is simply due to physical limitations, with a disk drive preventing full length cards from being fitted into these two slots. This is not a major drawback since many expansion cards are of the half length (or thereabouts) variety. It is not inconceivable that you would wish to have seven or eight full length boards in an XT, but it is a highly unlikely state of affairs. Note that some compatibles are capable of taking eight full length cards.

The 135 watt fan cooled power supply (usually 150 watts on clones) enables plenty of peripherals to be powered without any risk of overloading the supply unit. Originally the XT was supplied complete with a 10 megabyte hard disk drive, but this was later made an optional extra. A 20 megabyte hard disk option was also available. An optional 20 or 32 megabyte hard disk drive seems to be a standard option on all modern PC compatibles. Most manufacturers seem to offer several hard disk options, and there are plenty of do-it-yourself hard disk upgrade kits for floppy drive machines.

Turbo PCs

The computers in the IBM PC family are all based on microprocessors from the Intel 8086 series of microprocessors. The PC and PC XT computers are based on

8088, which is a slightly simplified version of the 8086. Whereas the 8086 has sixteen pins which carry data into and out of the device, the 8088 has only eight pins for this purpose. This means that the 8088 has to take in and put out 16 bit chunks of data or program instructions as two 8 bit chunks ("bytes"), one after the other. This is undesirable as it slows down the computer to a significant degree. Coupled with the relatively slow clock speed used in the PC and PC XT of just 4.77 MHz, this means that the standards PCs have little more computing power than the faster 8 bit computers.

As the PCs use the 8 bit data bus version of 16 bit 8086 microprocessor, it could be argued that they are in fact 8 bit computers and not genuine 16 bit types. Whether they are 8 or 16 bit machines, their computing performance is less than phenomenal, and with advances in computer hardware over the years they seem even less impressive these days than they did when they were launched.

IBM never produced what could really be regarded as a "turbo" version of the PC or PC XT. Most of the PC clones produced in recent years are of this type though, and there are three basic routes to obtaining increased speed. These can be used singly or in any combination. Details of the three methods are given below.

1. Increased Clock Speed
The most obvious way of obtaining increased operating speed is to use a higher clock frequency. It is an over-simplification to say that doubling the clock frequency doubles the speed of the computer, but in practice this is more or less what happens. In order to use a higher clock frequency successfully the microprocessor must obviously be able to run reliably at the higher frequency, as must the memory chips and other circuits in the computer. This puts definite limitations on the increase in speed that can be obtained using this method. Most clones used to operate at 8 MHz, but 10 MHz is now quite common. Some PC compatibles can operate at 12 MHz or even 15 MHz, giving a quite significant speed increase over the 4.77 MHz

versions. Turbo PCs usually give some means of switching the operating speed between the turbo speed and the standard 4.77 MHz clock rate.

In most cases there is no problem in using the higher speed, which brings only benefits. Some software can be difficult to use on fast PCs though, and some copy protected programs will not run properly in the turbo mode, or must be started with the computer set to the standard speed but can be run at full speed thereafter. There are various methods of speed switching, which include a hardware switch fitted to the computer, a program that provides this function, or speed switching incorporated in the ROM BIOS. With this last option pressing a certain combination of keys on the keyboard produces the speed change (pressing "Ctrl", "Alt" and "+" on the numeric keypad for example).

2. Using An 8086 Microprocessor

Using the 8086 with its 16 bit data bus might seem an obvious way of getting improved performance, but matters are not as simple as it might at first appear. The PCs have 8 bit expansion slots, making it difficult to obtain full hardware compatibility with them if the 16 bit 8086 is used. This problem is not insurmountable, and some 8086 based compatibles (notably some Amstrad and Olivetti machines) have been produced. This method of performance boosting is a relatively rare one though.

3. Using the NEC V20

The NEC V20 microprocessor is capable of undertaking all 8088 instructions, and is fully compatible with it. As a point of interest, it can also run all the instructions of the earlier 8080 8 bit microprocessor. The point about the V20 is that compared with the 8088 it takes fewer clock pulses to complete some instructions. This obviously gives a boost in speed, but not a vast one. It is difficult to give a figure for the increase in speed, as it obviously depends on the software being run, and whether or not it makes extensive use of the instructions that the V20 can run more quickly. From my experience and tests I would say that the increase was somewhere in the region of 20% to 30%. There is a V30 microprocessor, which is a stream-lined version of the 8086.

The V20 microprocessor was very popular with the clone manufacturers at one time, but its popularity waned somewhat when there was a copyright dispute involving this chip. This has now been resolved, and the V20 would seem to be coming back into fashion. In theory there should be no problems if an 8088 or 8086 chip is removed from a PC and replaced by a V20 or V30 type (as appropriate). I fitted a V30 chip in an Amstrad PC1512 computer some years ago, and have certainly never encountered any problems as a result of this changeover. The improvement in performance provided by this change is not vast, but as the V20 and V30 can be obtained at quite low prices, the increase is quite respectable for the cost involved.

PC AT Computers

Rather than trying to speed up the PC and PC XT, IBM produced what was effectively a completely new design, but one which largely maintained software and hardware compatibility with the PC and PC XT. This computer is the PC AT, and the "AT" part of the name stands for "advanced technology". This is based on the Intel 80286 microprocessor, which is an improved version of the 8086. Like the 8086 it has a 16 bit data bus, and the AT is therefore a true 16 bit computer.

The AT achieves higher operating speeds than the PC and PC XT because it operates at a higher clock speed. The original AT operates at 6 MHz, but the later versions have an 8 MHz clock. Comparing the speed of the PC and PC XT computers with the AT models is difficult since the 80286 takes fewer clock cycles per instruction than the 8086 or 8088. Thus, while it might seem as though a 10 MHz XT compatible is faster than a 6 MHz or 8 MHz AT, this is not actually the case. Popular methods of speed testing generally put the AT many times faster than

11

the original 4.77 MHz PC and PC XT machines. If you take the clock speed of an AT in MHz, then it is roughly that many times faster than a PC according to the popular speed tests.

In practical applications the difference in speed would often seem to be somewhat less than most speed tests would suggest. This is something that depends on the software in use, and is also governed to some extent by the particular peripheral devices fitted to the computer. Whatever method of speed testing you use though, the AT computers are certainly much faster than the PCs and PC XTs. Modern clones use higher clock speeds, with 10 MHz and (more commonly) 12 MHz or 12.5 MHz clock frequencies being the norm these days. There are plenty of ATs which operate at 16 MHz or even 20 MHz, making the original PCs look positively slow by comparison.

The original IBM AT computers were fitted with 512k of RAM on the motherboard, but all recent compatible machines would seem to be able to take the full 640k on the motherboard. In fact most AT computers can take at least 1 megabyte of memory on the main circuit board, and many are equipped to take 4 or 8 megabytes. These large amounts of RAM are made possible by an extra operating mode of the 80286 which takes advantage of extra address lines on the chip. However, when running PC/MS/DOS software the 80286 can not directly use the RAM above the 640k limit. This is not to say that there is no point in having the extra RAM. Some programs can use it in slightly roundabout methods, such as using the RAM for a disk cache or a RAM disk. Also, there are alternative operating systems such as OS/2 which can run programs in the mode which takes full advantage of the whole 16 megabyte address range.

As it is a true 16 bit computer, in order to take full advantage of the 16 bit data bus it needs to have 16 bit expansion slots. This obviously raises possibilities with incompatibility between the AT and existing 8 bit PC expansion cards. In order to minimise these problems the 16 bit expansion slots of the AT are in the form of standard

8 bit slots plus a second connector which carries the extra lines needed by 16 bit expansion boards. This means that any 8 bit card should work in an AT, with the only exception of boards which are PC or PC XT specific for some other reason. The only common example of this that springs to mind are the PC and PC XT hard disk controller cards. These have their own BIOS, whereas an AT hard disk controller card makes use of routines in the main BIOS on the motherboard. This gives what is really a firmware compatibility problem, rather than what could strictly speaking be termed hardware incompatibility.

Although an 8 bit card can usually be fitted to an AT computer, and in many cases ATs and PCs use the same 8 bit expansion cards, 16 bit cards are not necessarily suitable for use in PCs. There are some boards, such as some 16 bit VGA display cards, that will work in either type of computer. They sometimes achieve this by detecting electronically which type computer they are fitted in, and then configuring themselves accordingly. In other cases the user must set a switch on the card to the appropriate position. In most cases though, 16 bit cards are not usable in PC and PC XT machines. Where they can be used, they are likely to be operating at less than full capacity, and would probably represent an expensive solution to the problem. Note that not all the expansion slots in an AT computer are 16 bit types. In the original computers there are six 16 bit and two 8 bit slots. This is copied in most clones, but some AT compatibles seem to have five 16 bit and three 8 bit slots.

80386 ATs

When Intel produced an improved version of the 80286 microprocessor, the 80386, it was inevitable that this device would soon be used in a new and faster generation of PCs. This did indeed happen. For many years the 8088 based PCs were the most popular, but more recently the AT compatibles have held the largest share of the PC market, and most forecasts seem to point to 80386 computers taking over from the ATs in the not too distant future. With more and more software needing the power of the faster PCs in order to run well, and in some cases not being usable at all on PCs and PC XTs, the continuing rise in the popularity of the high-end PCs seems assured.

IBM never produced an 80386 based version of the PC. IBM have produced computers based on this microprocessor, but not in a straightforward PC guise. The new range of IBM microcomputers (the "PS/2" range) use a different form of expansion bus, and are discussed in more detail later on in this chapter. This lack of an IBM 80386 based PC to clone meant that the clone manufacturers were left without any standards to follow when producing 80386 PCs. Computers of this type are effectively AT clones, but using the 80386 plus its support chips instead of the 80286 and the relevant devices.

Using the 80386 in an AT style computer does have some advantages. The 80386 can operate with clock rates of up to at least 16 MHz, with 20 MHz, 25 MHz, and 33 MHz computers also being produced. I have often seen it stated that the 80386 can perform instructions in fewer clock cycles than the 80286, giving a vast increase in performance. On the other hand, the results of speed tests on various 80286 and 80386 computers would seem to suggest that there is little to choose between the two types of computer when running at the same clock rate. With some ATs running at a clock frequency of 20 MHz, and some 80386 computers operating at 16 MHz, the fastest ATs are faster at running standard PC software than are the slower 80386 computers.

The 80386 is a 32 bit microprocessor, which makes it potentially more powerful in maths intensive applications than the 16 bit 80286. However, to take advantage of this it is necessary to have software that is written specifically for the 32 bit 80386. Such software does exist, but at the moment it is decidedly "thin on the ground". Being a 32 bit microprocessor, the 80386 warrants a 32 bit expansion bus. Most ATs that are based on this device do have one or two 32 bit expansion slots, but the problem here is a lack of any true standardisation. Also, how many types of expansion board really need and could benefit from a 32 bit expansion bus? Probably not all that many, but it is largely of academic importance since there are so few 32 bit expansion boards available.

A number of computer manufacturers have got together to devise a 32 bit expansion slot standard which is an extension of the standard 8/16 bit type. The original expansion slot system is sometimes referred to as the "Industry Standard Architecture" type, or just "ISA". The new standard is called the "Enhanced Industry Standard Architecture" system, or "EISA" as it is better known. Whether or not this will go on to be a true standard remains to be seen.

Apart from its ability to access memory 32 bits at a time, the 80386 has other advantages in the way that it handles memory. For straightforward PC/MS/DOS applications it runs in the "real" mode (as does the 80286), and effectively just emulates the 8086. In the "protected virtual" mode (often just called "protected" mode) it is much like the 80286 in its mode which gives a 16 megabyte memory address range. It has some extensions in this mode though, including a memory management unit (MMU) which provides sophisticated memory paging and program switching capabilities. Perhaps of more immediate importance to most users, the 80386 can switch from the protected mode back to the real mode much more simply and quickly than the 80286 can manage. A program running in real mode, but making use of extended memory and protected mode via a RAM disk or whatever, will therefore operate more quickly when accessing the extended memory. This is not purely of academic importance, and some methods of using the extended memory on an 80386 based AT are not worthwhile when implemented on an 80286 based AT as they simply do not work fast enough.

The 80386 has a third mode of operation called "virtual real" mode. The 80286 has no equivalent of this mode. In essence it permits the memory to be split into several sections, with each one running its own operating system and an applications program. Each program is run entirely separately from the others, and if one program should crash then all the others should remain running normally. Only the crashed section of memory needs to have its operating system rebooted and the program reloaded. This solves what has tended to be a big problem with many multi-tasking computers, where programs tend to crash regularly due to one program interfering with another, and with one program crashed the whole system tends to follow suit. The amount of memory that the 80386 can handle is so large (4 gigabytes, or some 4000 megabytes in other words) that there is no immediate prospect of anyone manufacturing desktop computers that actually utilize a significant proportion of the available memory address range.

Clearly the 80386 is a formidable microprocessor, and any computer that uses one has great potential. As yet there is little software that fully exploits 80386 based AT style computers, but it seems likely that this situation will change in the fullness of time. There is certainly some impressive 80386 software starting to appear, but there is very little of it in evidence at the present time.

There is a sort of cut down version of the 80386, the 80386SX, which seems to be gaining in popularity as the basis for AT style PCs. This has a 16 bit bus like the 80286, but internally it has all the 80386 registers. This enables it to run 80386 specific software as well as standard PC software, albeit somewhat more slowly than on an 80386 based computer. The reduced speed is the result of the 32 bit pieces of data or instructions having to be loaded as two 16 bit chunks rather than being loaded simultaneously. There may seem to be little advantage in having an 80386SX computer at present, since they use clock rates of 16 MHz and 20 MHz, which means they are no faster than the best of the 80286 based AT computers. I suppose that the reason for their increasing popularity is that their cost is significantly less than a full 80386 based AT compatible, but they are better "future-proofed" than a standard AT or AT clone. In other words, there is

16

unlikely to be any PC software in the short to medium term that these computers can not run. Remember that the 80386SX has all the modes and capabilities of the 80386, but where 32 bit data transfers are required they must be undertaken as two 16 bit transfers, slowing things down slightly.

At the time of writing, Intel has recently started producing a new microprocessor in the 8086 series, the 80486. This is a very advanced chip which can significantly out-perform the 80386. Computers based on this device are starting to appear, but as yet they are very expensive. It seems likely that in due course the 80486 will have a significant effect on the PC compatible market, but as yet the cost of computers based on this chip is so high as to put them beyond the reach of most PC users.

PS/2 Computers

When IBM ceased making the PC range of computers they were replaced with the PS/2 range. This should perhaps be considered as two ranges, since it consists of relatively simple machines that could reasonably be regarded as modern PC compatibles, and a more advanced range which are still basically PCs, but which depart from the previous standards in some quite radical ways.

The most basic of the PS/2 range are the Model 25 and the Model 30. These are 8 MHz 8086 based computers which use standard ISA expansion slots of the 8 bit variety. They differ from earlier PCs in that they have a number of functions (such as the display generator circuitry) on the motherboard rather than requiring these functions to be provided by cards fitted in expansion slots. There is also a Model 30 286 computer, which is a 10 MHz 80286 based computer having 16 bit ISA expansion slots. The Model 25/30 and Model 30 286 computers are effectively the modern equivalents of the XT and AT computers, and are PCs in the generally accepted sense of the term.

The Model 50, 60, 70, and 80 computers are more advanced computers which use a different form of expansion bus called "micro channel architecture", or just "MCA" as it is much better known. This is not really the place for a discussion of this expansion bus standard, since the subject of this book is the expansion of what for the want of a better term we will call the traditional PC. The subject of MCA will therefore not be considered any further here.

System Make Up
A traditional PC is a so-called three unit style computer. These three separate units are the keyboard, the main computer unit, and the monitor. They are connected together by cables, with a curly type normally being used for the keyboard. This is a convenient setup in that it makes it easy to accommodate everything on practically any computer desk. Bear in mind though, that PCs are mostly quite large and heavy, and likely to prove both too big and too heavy for a low cost computer desk designed for a small home computer.

The main unit is comprised of several sub-units. The main ones are the case, power supply unit, motherboard, and one or more disk drives. Additionally, certain expansion cards must be present on the main board for the system to function. These are a floppy disk controller and a display generator to drive the monitor. If a hard disk is installed, then this will require a suitable controller, which in some cases will also act as the controller for the floppy disk drive or drives. A practical system will almost certainly need input/output ports to enable it to operate with such things as mice, printers, plotters, modems, etc. Serial and parallel ports are provided by one or more expansion cards. A basic PC would therefore consist of something like the following list of main parts.

Keyboard
Case
Motherboard fitted with BIOS and memory chips
Monochrome monitor

Monochrome display card
Floppy disk drive
Floppy disk drive controller
Serial/parallel port card

A more up-market PC might have the following set of main components.

Keyboard
Case
Motherboard fitted with BIOS and memory chips
Multisync Colour Monitor
High resolution colour graphics display card
Twin floppy disk drives
Hard disk drive
Twin floppy and hard disk controller card
Serial/parallel port card
Second serial port card
Expanded memory board card

Some of these constitute parts, plus more specialised forms of expansion, are discussed in later chapters, but there are a few aspects of these main parts which we will take the opportunity to discuss here.

Keyboards

The original PC keyboard, and one which is still available today, is a 83 key type. At least it is in its native (U.S.A.) form. The U.K. version has a slightly different layout plus an extra key in order to accommodate the pound sign ("£"), which is absent on the U.S.A. keyboard. The U.K. version is therefore generally known as the 84 key layout PC keyboard. This has ten function keys in two vertical rows of five, positioned to the left of the main QWERTY keys.

To the right of this main section there is a combined cursor key cluster and numeric keypad. Normally keys "8", "2", "4", and "6" operate as the up, down, left, and right cursor keys respectively. However, if the "Num

Lock" key is operated, these keys then operate as appropriate number keys of the numeric keypad. The "Num Lock" key is a toggle type, which means that operating it again switches the keys back to cursor operation, pressing it again sets them to numeric operation, and so on. Other keys on the numeric keypad have alternative functions when "Num Lock" is off, such as the "1" and "7" keys which are "End" and "Home" when "Num Lock" is off.

A PC keyboard is quite a sophisticated piece of electronics in its own right, and is actually based on an 8048 single chip microprocessor (or "micro controller" as these devices are alternatively known). This controller provides "debouncing", which prevents multiple characters being generated if the keyboard switches open and close something less than completely cleanly (which is always the case in practice). The keyboard controller also performs simple diagnostic tests, and can detect a key that is stuck in the "on" position for example. It also contains a 20 byte buffer, which is simply a small amount of memory that is used to store characters if one key is pressed before the character from the previous one has been read by the computer.

The keyboard also has multi-character roll-over. In other words, if you press one key, and then another while still holding down the first one, the second key will be read correctly. In fact you can hold down several keys and the next one that is operated will still be read correctly. I do not know how many keys can be pressed before this system breaks down, but attempts to overload the keyboard on my AT compatible proved to be fruitless. Of course, like most computer keyboards and electric typewriters, the keyboard includes an auto-repeat function (i.e. holding down any character key results in that character being produced once initially, and then after a short delay it is repeated for as long as the key is pressed).

Connection to the computer is via a five way cable fitted with a 5 way 180 degree DIN plug. This is a form of serial interface, and the standard method of connection is shown in Figure 1.1. Note that although PCs (including

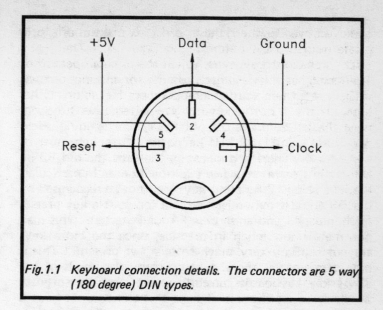

Fig.1.1 Keyboard connection details. The connectors are 5 way (180 degree) DIN types.

PC XTs) and AT computers both have the same connector and method of connection, they use slightly different methods of interfacing to the computer. This means that a PC keyboard is unusable with an AT, and vice versa. Most of the keyboards on sale these days seem to be switchable between PC and AT operation, and I have encountered one or two which sense the type of computer they are connected to and automatically switch to the appropriate mode of operation.

Most PC compatibles are currently supplied with keyboards having the enhanced layout that was introduced by IBM in 1986. This has 101 keys in its original U.S.A. version, or 102 keys in the case of the U.K. version. The ten function keys of the original design are replaced by twelve function keys on the enhanced layout. These keys are relocated to a single row above the main QWERTY keyboard (which is where the "Esc" key is also to be found). The numeric keypad/cursor key arrangement is retained, but only for those who are used to the original scheme of things and wish to go on using it. This keypad

21

is moved over to the right in order to make room for a separate cursor cluster etc.

The enhanced keyboards retain the original method of interfacing, and it is quite possible, for instance, to use a 102 key AT keyboard as a replacement for an 84 key AT type. This will not necessarily give perfect results though, since the BIOS in the computer may not be equipped to deal with a 101/102 key keyboard. Although most of the keys are merely duplicating those of the old 83/84 key layout, there are a few additional ones. In particular, the F11 and F12 function keys may not be recognised by the BIOS, or it may mistake them for double key presses (shift plus F3 and shift plus F4 for instance). This may not matter too much in practice, since the extra keys are not used by very much software at present. This is not surprising, as there must be many thousands of the 83/84 key keyboards currently in use, and any software which relies on the use of keys that they do not have is likely to cause considerable consumer dissatisfaction. Where these extra keys can be utilized, there are usually alternatives which use the keys present on the 83/84 key keyboards.

A strange problem can arise with the num lock function when using an enhanced keyboard with a computer that has a BIOS which is intended for operation with the original style of keyboard. What should happen is for the BIOS to send a signal to the keyboard during the start-up routine that sets num lock on. Computer manufacturers often supply a "NUMLOCK.COM" program with their computers, which can be run from the "AUTOEXEC.BAT" file if it is preferred that the computer should start with the num lock function switched off. What can happen with a computer that has an unsuitable BIOS is that the num lock function is left switched off. Operating the "Num Lock" key switches it on alright, but confusingly, the num lock light fails to switch on. Pressing the "Num Lock" key twice more restores normal operation. I have never found a solution to this minor niggle, other than fitting a more modern BIOS chip or chips that is.

A more serious problem when upgrading from an 83/84 key keyboard to a 101/102 key type is that some of the keys will not produce the correct characters. Often the "#" key produces the "\" character, and the "\" key has no effect at all. Since the "\" character is an important one for changing directories, specifying paths, etc., this can be quite awkward if no means of correcting it is found. Computers that are supplied complete with enhanced keyboards usually have a program which can be run from the "AUTOEXEC.BAT" file at switch-on, and which does any necessary remapping of the keyboard. The Dell System 200 computer I used to produce this book for instance, came complete with a program called "KEY102" which provides this function. If you can legitimately get hold of a program of this type, it represents the easiest solution to the problem. Unfortunately, I am not aware of any programs of this type which are sold commercially, or are available through shareware/PD distributors.

An alternative is to use one of the many keyboard remapping programs that are available. These mostly offer facilities that go well beyond simple keyboard remapping, but in most cases you can ignore the "bells and whistles" features and just use the programs for simple remapping purposes. A problem with these programs is that they do not always work properly with "foreign" keyboards, and foreign in this case means any non-U.S.A. keyboard, which obviously includes 102 key U.K. types. The only way to ascertain whether or not a program of this type will do what you want is to try it and see. There are several PD/shareware programs of this type, and the "try before you buy" approach obviously has a great deal to be said for it under these circumstances. Most keyboards can be remapped successfully, although it might take a little thought and careful planning of the order in which the keys are remapped.

The only insurmountable keyboard remapping problem I have encountered was with an AT computer which had a

BIOS that did not seem to recognise the 102nd key (the one marked "\" and "|") at all. This was a bit surprising as the BIOS was a very modern one. It was presumably a case of the BIOS only being designed for the American market and the U.S.A. style 101 key keyboard, rather than the BIOS being out of date. If the BIOS does not recognise a key code, then I think I am right in saying that no key remapping will do so either. Certainly with the AT compatible in question a whole series of keyboard utility programs failed to recognise any presses of the extra key. The only solution was to fit the computer with a different BIOS.

Motherboards

Unless you get into DIY PC assembly or repairs you may not need to know too much about motherboards, although background information of this type often proves to be invaluable from time to time. Motherboards can be broadly broken down into two main categories; the PC/PC XT type, and the AT type. This second category can be further broken down into two types: the 80286 and 80386 boards. In terms of their physical characteristics, the PC XT boards are smaller and have the mounting holes positioned slightly differently to the AT boards. More recent AT boards have been cut down in size slightly, but have retained the mounting arrangement of the original in order to maintain compatibility.

The situation is confused by the fact that manufacturers of the clone motherboards have tended to make further reductions in the size of their boards, although they invariably seem to retain the standard mounting arrangements so that their boards will readily fit into standard PC cases. The standard PC XT board has three rows of three mounting holes, but a modern miniature board would typically be only about two-thirds as deep as the original XT boards, and would only have two rows of mounting holes. It is the front part of the board that is omitted, since the rear section carries the expansion slots and must be present. With a smaller board fewer mounting screws are needed in order to fix the board firmly in place, and the missing holes are of no consequence.

With AT boards there was originally a trend towards narrower boards. This was probably to reduce manufacturing costs, but narrower boards are generally easier to deal with when assembling and servicing AT type computers. With the original full size boards, a substantial area of the board was positioned in rather inaccessible places under the power supply unit and the disk drives. With the modern narrow variety it is quite common for little or none of the board to be tucked away under the power supply or disk drives. Most of the more recent AT clone motherboards seem to be PC XT size, often with provision for mounting in both PC XT and AT style cases. This may seem a strange development, but the idea was probably to make it possible for owners of old PC XT or compatible computers to upgrade their computers to AT compatibles by replacing the original motherboard with one of these new units.

It would be an exaggeration to say that it is merely a matter of swopping over the motherboards and reconnecting all the expansion cards and peripherals in order to convert an XT into an AT. There are a few complications which have to be sorted out. One problem is that AT computers have higher capacity floppy disks than do XT computers (1.2 megabyte as opposed to 360k or 0.36 megabytes). This does not necessarily matter too much, as the AT board's BIOS might support 360k drives, and the computer might work with 360k drives. A more severe problem is that AT hard disk controllers are 16 bit boards, and use the BIOS on the motherboard. XT hard disk controllers are 8 bit boards and have an on-board BIOS. This makes them totally incompatible, and a new hard disk controller is essential if upgrading from an XT to an AT. This subject will not be pursued further here since disk drives are covered in some detail in their own chapter.

Configuration

For the computer to function properly it must know a few basic facts about itself, such as the type of display card and amount of memory fitted. This ensures that it produces an initial display properly, that it does not try to access memory it does not have, or ignore memory that it does have available. The methods of setting up this configuration information so that the computer can use it are totally different for the PC/PC XT computers and the AT machines. PC XT motherboards have a set of switches that must be set to the appropriate settings. The AT computers have some low power memory which is powered from a battery when the main power source is switched off. This memory circuit is actually part of a built-in clock/calendar circuit which DOS uses to set its clock and calendar during the booting process.

There is no direct PC or PC XT equivalent to this, since the clock/calendar on these computers is an optional extra provided by an expansion card. These cards are supplied complete with utility programs that pass on the time and date to DOS, and enable the time and date to be set by the user. As many users, including myself, have discovered, you are unlikely to be able to use these boards if they are not supplied together with the necessary utility programs! One or two manufacturers (notably Amstrad with the 1512 series) have used the battery backed memory of the clock/calendar circuit to store configuration information on XT compatibles, but this is a non-standard approach, and one which again relies on suitable utility software being supplied with the computer.

We will consider the PC and compatible computers first. The motherboard has two banks of DIP (dual-in-line plastic) switches, with eight switches in each bank. Figure 1.2 shows the functions of these switches. This method is now obsolete, and was replaced by a single DIP switch when the XT was introduced. The functions of the eight configuration switches of the XT board are shown in Figure 1.3.

Switch 1 is always set to the off position, while switch

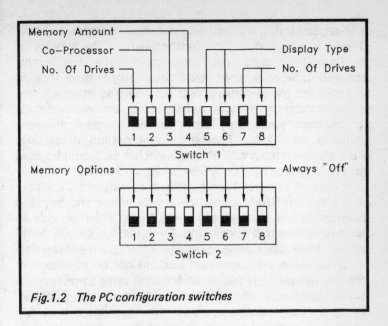

Fig.1.2 The PC configuration switches

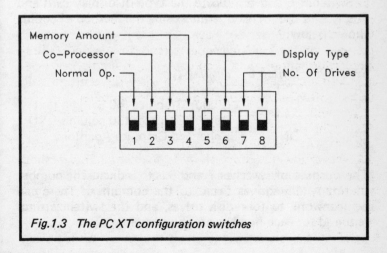

Fig.1.3 The PC XT configuration switches

2 is set to "on" if no maths co-processor is fitted, or "off" if one is installed on the motherboard. The subject of maths co-processors is discussed more fully later in this chapter. The amount of RAM fitted on the motherboard is indicated by switches 3 and 4. The way in which this operates tends to vary somewhat from one motherboard to another, since they are designed to take different amounts of RAM. Typically, combinations of settings from both switches off to both switches on would be used for RAM amounts of 0k, 256k, 512k, and 640k.

A few XT compatible boards are equipped to take 1 megabyte of RAM. This is usually where the board is designed to use 1 megabyte RAM chips, which provide an economic means of providing the basic 640k DOS RAM even if some 384k is left unused. The extra RAM is usually available to the computer, but can not be addressed in the normal way. It has to be accessed using some form of paging technique, and is not available for normal DOS use. Computers and motherboards which have this extra RAM are normally supplied with some software that enables it to be utilized indirectly by applications programs. Typical utilities of this type would be RAM disk and printer spooler programs.

Switches 5 and 6 indicate the type of display card and monitor in use. This operates using the method of coding shown below:—

Switch 5	Switch 6	Display type
OFF	OFF	Monochrome
OFF	ON	Colour Graphics (40 column text)
ON	OFF	Colour Graphics (80 column text)
ON	ON	Enhanced Graphics Adaptor

The purpose of switches 7 and 8 is to indicate the number of floppy disk drives fitted to the computer. There can be from one to four disk drives, and the switch settings required for each number are shown below:—

Switch 7	Switch 8	Number of disk drives
ON	ON	One drive
OFF	ON	Two drives
ON	OFF	Three drives
ON	ON	Four drives

Although the PCs were originally designed to handle up to four disk drives, modern clones can not usually be used with more than two floppy drives. Or to be more accurate, they can not normally be used with more than two floppy disk drives except by adopting methods that make it hardly worth the effort of doing so. All the PC floppy disk controllers I have encountered are capable of handling twin floppy drives, but no more than this. Even if the floppy disk controller card can handle four disk drives, it is by no means certain that the computer's BIOS will be able to do so. With the relatively low cost of 20 megabyte hard disk drives these days, there would seem to be little point in equipping a PC with masses of floppy disk drives anyway. A single or twin floppy system plus a hard disk drive would seem to be a much better way of spending the money, and should satisfy most requirements.

AT Setup
As already explained, configuration information is stored in AT computers in a different manner. A 6818 clock/calendar chip (or equivalent circuitry) is a standard part of the AT motherboard. This device has a very low power consumption that enables it to be powered by a battery when the computer is switched off and power is not available from the mains power supply. The battery supply is often in the form of a nickel-cadmium rechargeable type which is trickle charged when the computer is switched on. Provided the computer is not left unused for long periods of time, this ensures that the clock/calendar circuit does not suffer from amnesia.

An alternative is to have ordinary dry batteries (typically four HP7 size cells) which are replaced about every six months or so. This system might include an on-board battery of some kind which keeps the clock/calendar powered while the main batteries are changed. Even if it does, there is still a risk of the clock/calendar losing its supply before the main batteries are changed, with everything having to be reset as a result.

A third method is to have a clock/calendar circuit which has an extremely low current consumption indeed, with a long-life lithium battery providing the power. The battery will normally be guaranteed to operate for about five years or more, so that it could outlast the computer! However, if the computer is well looked after and properly serviced, the battery will eventually have to be changed, and the clock/calendar will need to be set up properly again.

In addition to the clock/calendar circuit the 6818 contains 50 bytes of low power CMOS RAM which is also powered from the backup battery. It is in this memory that the configuration information is contained. This memory is not part of the normal complement of RAM, and does not appear in the computer's memory map. The 6818 is, like the serial ports, parallel ports, etc., in the separate input/output map. The addresses set aside for the clock/calendar etc. are from 070 to 07F, but only addresses 070 and 071 are actually used. The first address is fed with a number from 0 to 63, which selects the required register or memory location of the 6818. Address 071 is then used to read data from, or write data to, the selected clock register or byte of memory. The first fourteen addresses are used for the clock/calendar's registers, while the remaining fifty are used for the memory.

It is quite easy to use GW BASIC to read and alter the contents of the 6818. Reading the contents of this device will do no harm, but writing to it and tinkering with the data it contains is not a good idea. You could easily find that mistakes result in problems when trying to use the disk drives, with the computer perhaps refusing to acknowledge that the hard disk drive exists. There is probably some risk of data on disks (including the hard disk) being lost if the computer is used while it has incorrect configuration information in the battery backed memory. Due to the potential for users getting the configuration data wrong, and the possible consequences, some AT type computer manufacturers have been reluctant to supply the setup program with their AT machines. The idea is that dealers should correctly configure the computer for users before delivery, and should undertake any necessary resetting or reconfiguration that might become necessary in due course.

This system tends not to be very popular with the end-users. If the data in the 6818 should become corrupted for some reason, the computer might be out of commission for some time before the dealer puts matters right. It might even be necessary for the computer to be returned to the dealer for reconfiguration. Since a standard AT is far from portable, this would probably be a difficult and expensive business. If the user should upgrade the computer, such as adding an extra disk drive or a better display adapter, it would be necessary to have the dealer change the information in the battery backed RAM before the improved hardware could be used.

Presumably due to consumer resistance, most AT type computers now seem to be supplied with a suitable setup program. This may be in the form of a program supplied on a floppy disk, but quite often the setup program is contained in the BIOS ROMs. On the computer I am using to produce this book, for instance, pressing the "Ctrl", "Alt", and "Return" keys simultaneously results in the setup program being run, and a list of options being displayed on the screen. This is mostly straight-forward, with the desired display type etc. being selected from lists of options using the cursor keys and the Return key, or some similar arrangement. You do not need to know about the values needed at each memory location for a given set of hardware — the program works all this out for you and places the appropriate values into the CMOS RAM.

The exception is when specifying hard disk drive types. Originally there were just fifteen types of hard disk that were supported by the ROM BIOS. In fact this is not quite true, since the drive types are from 1 to 15, but type 15 is "reserved", and only fourteen different drive configurations are actually supported by early AT BIOS ROMs. Modern BIOSs generally support forty or more different hard disk types. With some BIOSs you need to know which type number your drive corresponds to, since they deal only in these numbers and give no real help. With others, as you scroll through the various type numbers that are supported, the setup program displays some basic information about the drive that corresponds to each number. This information generally includes at least the number of heads and the number of tracks ("cylinders") per head. It is a good idea to run the setup program on a newly acquired AT style computer so that you can make a note of the hard disk type, just in case you need to restore the contents of the CMOS RAM at some later time.

Some BIOS programs are quite advanced, and will spot any inconsistencies between the configuration information in the CMOS RAM and the actual hardware present. When the setup program is run it will then automatically supply itself with the correct information (with manual override available just in case the program makes a mistake)! This would seem to obviate the need for the CMOS RAM, since the BIOS can discover what hardware is present without its help. Presumably the CMOS RAM must still be present in case some applications software should refer to it in order to ascertain some facts about the computer's configuration. Otherwise, it would seem to serve no useful purpose with an advanced BIOS of this type.

For the record, this is a list of the functions provided by each register/RAM location of the 6818 in an AT style computer. Note that there may be some variation from one AT clone to another, but all the ATs I have used have closely adhered to this scheme of things.

Address	Function
00	Seconds
01	Seconds Alarm
02	Minutes
03	Minutes Alarm
04	Hours
05	Hours Alarm
06	Day Of Week
07	Day Of Month
08	Month
09	Year
0A	Status Register A
0B	Status Register B
0C	Status Register C
0D	Status Register D
0E	Diagnostic Status Byte
0F	Shutdown
10	Disk Drive Type (A and B)
11	Reserved
12	Fixed Drive Type (C and D)
13	Reserved
14	Equipment Byte
15	Low Base Memory
16	High Base Memory
17	Low Expansion Memory
18	High Expansion Memory
19 to 2D	Reserved
2E & 2F	CMOS Checksum
30	Low Expansion Memory
31	High Expansion Memory
32	Data Century
33	Information Flags (set at power-up)
34 to 3F	Reserved

Maths Co-Processor

A maths co-processor is an integrated circuit, which looks very much like the main microprocessor in most cases. It is not normally fitted via an expansion card, but instead fits into a socket on the motherboard. I do not know if all

PC compatibles are equipped with such a socket, but I have never come across one that did not have it. Even a lot of the PC compatible portable and luggable computers seem to have a socket for a maths co-processor.

Whether or not you need to fit one of these components depends on the software you are running. Applications programs such as word processors which do not undertake a lot of complex mathematics will not be written to take advantage of a maths co-processor, and will not benefit at all if one is fitted. It is important to realise that only programs that are specifically written to exploit a maths co-processor will actually make use of it.

The programs that are most likely to take advantage of a co-processor are the ones which undertake large amounts of complex calculation. This mainly means spreadsheets and CAD (computer aided drawing) programs. The only way to discover whether or not your programs can take advantage of a co-processor is to consult the manuals. By no means all programs that might benefit from one are actually written to do so. At the other extreme, some programs, particularly CAD types, can only be used in a computer which is fitted with a maths co-processor. In some instances software is supplied in two versions — one to be used if a co-processor is fitted, and the other to be used if it is not.

The increase in performance provided by a co-processor is totally dependent on the applications program. The greater the amount of advanced mathematics that it undertakes, the greater the potential advantage of using a co-processor. However, how well (or otherwise) the program is designed to exploit the co-processor must also be taken into account. A speed increase by a factor of fifty to seventy times is supposed to be achievable, but you should bear in mind that no practical program is purely advanced mathematics. The actual speed increase is therefore likely to be much more modest in practice. An increase in speed by a factor of ten would be extremely good, and in practice most programs seem to fall significantly short of this. One CAD program I used seem to only speed up by about

30% when provided with a maths co-processor.

As these components are quite expensive, you really need to be reasonably sure that fitting one will actually provide an improvement in performance before actually buying one. On the other hand, where a program will take good advantage of this component, it represents what must be considered a very cost effective means of providing a worthwhile improvement in speed.

The type of maths co-processor you need depends on the type of microprocessor used in your PC. The computers that are based on the 8088 or 8086 (i.e. PCs, PC XTs, and compatibles) require the 8087. There is more than one version of the 8087, but they differ only in the maximum clock speed that they can handle. With this type of maths co-processor the speed of the co-processor should be equal to or higher than the clock speed of the computer. Thus, for a 8 MHz XT compatible you would use the 8 MHz version of the 8087. The 10 MHz version would also be perfectly acceptable, but as the versions that can handle higher clock rates cost more than the slower versions, it is an unnecessary expense to use a faster version than is really necessary.

These days there is a tendency to cut costs by using devices beyond their specifications. This seems to be done with microprocessors, maths co-processors, and memory chips. It is not only do-it-yourself upgraders that sometimes resort to this practice. There are plenty of computers, motherboards, etc., that are sold complete with components that are run at speeds which are beyond their rated maximums. This does not result in the degree of unreliability that one might expect. In fact, in most cases it will provide perfectly satisfactory results. I have quite successfully used an 8 MHz 8087 removed from an old XT compatible in a new one operating at a clock frequency of 10 MHz. The computer I am using to produce this book can run its maths co-processor at 8 MHz or 12 MHz, and although I have an 8 MHz component, I have no problems if I run it at 12 MHz.

The reason that you can often get away with this type

of thing is that semiconductors such as memory chips and microprocessors are tested at speeds significantly beyond their rated maximums. This is to give the manufacturers a generous safety margin, so that there is no significant risk of them being bothered by complaints from users who experience occasional glitches from components that are run close to their maximum speed ratings.

You can save money by using components beyond their maximum speed ratings, and you might obtain trouble-free operation. You will be running the equipment with a safety margin that is very slim though, and in some cases occasional or even frequent glitches might be the result. The consequences of slight malfunctions might not be very great, or they might be disastrous. You have to decide for yourself whether or not the lower cost is worth the reduced reliability. If in doubt, always use components within their speed rating. It is perhaps worth pointing out that in general the power consumption of logic integrated circuits increases as their operating frequency is raised. When using a component beyond its rated maximum operating frequency there is just a slight risk that it will draw so much power that it will overheat.

For an 80286 based computer (i.e. a standard AT type) an 80287 maths co-processor is required. Like the 8087, the 80287 is available in several versions, with the maximum operating frequency being the only difference between them. Selecting the right version of an 80287 can be a bit confusing, as it operates asynchronously with the main processor. In other words, they are not necessarily operated at the same clock frequency. When I first bought a 12 MHz "turbo" AT compatible I searched for some time in an attempt to obtain a 12 MHz maths co-processor for it. In fact, no such component existed at that time, and the choice was between 6 MHz, 8 MHz, and 10 MHz components. The correct version for my 12 MHz AT was a 6 MHz type!

As pointed out above, an 80287 does not have to operate at the same speed as the 80286 microprocessor, and in most AT style computers it does not. In keeping with the original IBM AT computers, most AT clones operate their maths co-processor chips at two-thirds of the main clock speed. This is about 5.3 MHz for an 8 MHz AT, and in the case of my AT mentioned above it retained this maths co-processor clock rate even when set to the "turbo" mode. This is unusual, and most modern clones seem to use a co-processor clock rate that is always about two-thirds of the main clock rate (a clock rate of 7.5 MHz or 8 MHz seems to be normal for 12 MHz and 12.5 MHz AT clones).

The situation is complicated by the fact that some ATs enable the maths co-processor clock rate to be set independently of the main processor clock rate. On the Dell System 200 computer I am using to produce this book, the built-in setup program includes a facility to enable switching the maths co-processor between 8 MHz and 12 MHz.

In order to determine the correct version for your particular computer, it is necessary to refer to the manual, or if that fails to give the required information, enquire at the dealer where you purchased the computer. There is at least one public domain maths co-processor speed testing program available, but software of this type is of limited help. It will only run if the maths co-processor is fitted. It can tell you whether or not your co-processor is running at a speed that is within its maximum rating, but it will not tell you the clock speed before you have bought and fitted one.

An alternative to using a straightforward 80287 is to use one which is fitted on a small printed circuit board (often called a "daughter board"), and has its own crystal oscillator to set the operating speed. A device of this type plugs into the motherboard in the normal way, and as they are only fractionally larger than an ordinary maths co-processor it is unlikely that there will be any difficulty in fitting one. With one of these units you do not need to worry about speed ratings, because the on-board oscillator will, of course, operate at a frequency that is within the capabilities of the maths co-processor chip.

A maths co-processor unit of this type is more expensive than a standard 80287, but it offers performance advantages when used with computers that only enable the co-processor to be run at relatively low frequencies. Taking an extreme example, a 6 MHz AT would operate the co-processor at just 4 MHz, whereas a unit having a built-in clock oscillator would typically operate at 8 MHz or 10 MHz. This clearly gives a great speed advantage. Of course, in an AT that permits the co-processor to run at about 10 MHz anyway there is no point in using a unit of this type, unless it is one of the new generation that provides operating speeds beyond 10 MHz. The main problem with any of these units that include an on-board oscillator is that they are difficult to track down. Most computer equipment suppliers only offer 80287s which do not include a built-in clock oscillator.

80386 based ATs often have provision for both an 80287 and an 80387. The latter is the correct co-processor for operation with an 80386 based computer. Early 80386 AT motherboards were often equipped to take the 80287 as this chip was much cheaper and more readily available at that time. This feature is retained in many of the more recent 80386 motherboards, but it seems to be much less common than it once was. The cost of 80387s is relatively low these days, and they are much easier to obtain. This makes using an 80287, with its low level of performance, a much less attractive proposition than it once was. Of course, where sockets for both types are fitted, you should only fit one device or the other, not both. With the 80387 it is standard practice to use a device which has the same speed rating as the 80386 main processor. Like the 8087, it runs asynchronously with the main processor.

The 80386SX based computers require an 80387SX maths co-processor. At the time of writing this, both the 80386SX and the 80387SX only seem to be produced in 16 MHz versions, and there is no need to worry about different versions.

There should be no difficulty in locating the socket on

the motherboard for the maths co-processor, since it is highly unlikely that there will be another socket having the right number of terminals (forty or more in two rows). Any other integrated circuit holders will probably have only sixteen or eighteen terminals (again in two rows) and will be intended for memory chips. All the co-processor chips mentioned here are static sensitive types, and are vulnerable to damage by high static voltages. The manufacturers often list recommendations about the environment etc. when handling these chips, and these often involve the use of special static-free chambers and other high-tech (and high price) equipment that few will have access to.

From my quite considerable experience of handling static sensitive components it would seem that the risks of chips being accidentally "zapped" are often greatly exaggerated. Provided you avoid handling the components near any obvious sources of static electricity, and do not wear any clothes that are known to be prone to static generation, it is highly unlikely that there will be any problems. On the other hand, you may prefer to let a dealer fit the component and take the risk of the chip being damaged by static charges in the environment. This will almost certainly cost substantially more than buying the chip from a mail order company or other "cash and carry" outfit, but it might be worth the extra money for your peace of mind.

If you should decide to fit the chip yourself, there are a few points to bear in mind. First, and most important, it must be fitted the right way round. The pins of an integrated circuit are numbered in the manner shown in Figure 1.4, which shows a top view of the component. There are various ways in which the end of the component which has pin 1 can be indicated, and these are all shown in Figure 1.4. You should find that the pin numbers are marked on the motherboard, or that the manual for your computer shows the correct orientation for the device. Some computers now seem to come complete with a little map, usually fitted on top of the power supply unit

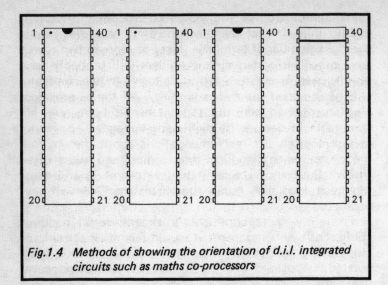

Fig.1.4 *Methods of showing the orientation of d.i.l. integrated circuits such as maths co-processors*

or the hard disk drive, which shows the location of the major components. This, if fitted, may well show the correct orientation for the device.

If in any doubt, do not fit the component yourself — get a dealer to do it. Fitting the co-processor round the wrong way will almost certainly result in its destruction. With maths co-processors costing around £100.00 to £500.00 it is clearly not worthwhile taking any risks.

Integrated circuits, even the smaller ones, are notoriously difficult to fit into holders. With the larger ones, which certainly includes all the 8087 series co-processors, things are especially difficult. The problem stems from the fact that as supplied, the two rows of pins are slightly splayed apart. This makes it difficult to fit the device manually, but apparently makes life easier for automated production systems. Those who are experienced at fitting integrated circuits often use a method which basically consists of semi-inserting one row of pins, then squeezing the second row into position, and then finally pushing the device fully into the socket. For those who are not used to dealing with these components it is much safer to bend all the pins inwards slightly before trying to fit it in place. Trying to push them inwards with your fingers is not a good idea, as you will almost certainly push some further in than others. The usual technique is to firmly hold the device with the pins placed flat against a table-top, and to then bend the pins inwards by tilting the body of the component in the appropriate direction. This is then repeated for the second row of pins.

With the bends in the pins at something close to right angles, the integrated circuit should fit into place without too much difficulty. Push it gently into place initially, getting all the pins partially in place, and checking that it is the right way round. Push it fully down into the socket only when you are completely sure that none of the pins are starting to buckle under the device, or are slipping outside the socket. If a pin should start to buckle, gently prise the component free using a small screwdriver, straighten out the offending pin, and try again to insert the component into the holder.

With 80387 maths co-processors you will find that the chip does not have pins. Instead it will be a square device with numerous metal contacts on the underside. This type of integrated circuit simply drops into the socket, and a metal clip (which is part of the socket) is then pulled into position to hold the chip in place. Three corners of the devices have notches, and this is a simple method of ensuring that the component can not be fitted into the socket the wrong way round.

Remember that if your computer is a PC, PC XT, or compatible, the appropriate switch on the motherboard must have its setting changed when the maths co-processor has been fitted. It must be pointed out that not all XT compatibles have this switch. When I fitted a maths co-processor to an Amstrad PC1512 computer, there seemed to be no switch or jumper lead settings to alter, and simply fitting the maths co-processor gave perfectly satisfactory results. If your computer does not have the standard XT DIP switches, then you should check the manual to determine whether or not there are any switches or jumper leads that need to be altered.

With an AT computer you may need to use the setup program to let the computer know that a maths co-processor is fitted, or you may find that the BIOS automatically detects its presence with no manual interference being required. You may find that an AT computer needs switches or jumper lead settings altered when a co-processor is fitted. I think that I am right in saying that in theory no switches or jumpers should be required. In practice an empty maths co-processor socket can cause problems, and in some ATs it must be cut off from the computer's busses unless the co-processor is actually installed. To determine whether or not this is the case you should consult the computer's manual, or if it has the "map" of the computer mentioned previously, this should point out any switches or jumper blocks associated with the co-processor.

Some maths co-processors are supplied complete with test software, or you may be able to find something of this type in a catalogue of PD/shareware software. The "acid test" is to try running an applications program that requires a maths co-processor. You will soon find out if the co-processor is not performing properly!

Ports
While it is not inconceivable that a computer could be put to good use without the aid of printers, modems, and other peripheral devices, few people can utilize one in this way. Unless you are using a computer for an application where there will be no need to produce any hard copy, or transfer data via means other than swapping floppy disks, at least one parallel or serial port will be required. Some modern PCs have a serial and a parallel port built-in, with the necessary hardware included on the motherboard. Connection to the outside world is via sockets mounted on the rear of the casing (most cases have holes for standard D type connectors ready cut), or mounted on expansion slot blanking plates. It is quite common for

display adaptors to include a parallel port, particularly CGA, and Hercules types. It is something that is often absent on EGA and VGA type display cards though.

The usual way of providing the parallel and serial ports is via expansion cards that offer one or more of these ports. A typical PC compatible would be supplied with two parallel and one serial port, with the first parallel port being provided by the display adaptor. The other two ports would then be provided by a parallel/serial adaptor card. However, this is just one common arrangement, and there are numerous other combinations in use. Probably for many users the ports supplied as standard will suffice. Most computers are connected to a printer, usually via a parallel port. This is the only peripheral used with many computer systems though.

A mouse (or other pointing device such as a digitising tablet or tracker ball) is now virtually a standard PC peripheral, and these can be of either the bus or serial varieties. A bus mouse is supplied complete with an expansion card which interfaces the mouse to the computer. A serial mouse connects to a standard serial port. On the face of it a bus mouse is the better option, as it leaves the serial port free for other purposes. In practice matters are not necessarily as clear cut as this. There is a slight risk of a bus mouse conflicting with other hardware, and a bus mouse is sometimes more expensive.

Probably the main potential problem with a bus mouse is that not all software that supports a mouse actually uses the driver program supplied with the mouse. This driver is either a .COM program that is run before using any applications software that requires the mouse driver, or a .SYS program that is run at switch-on from the CONFIG.SYS file. In either case the driver operates in the background while the applications program is running. There are many applications programs, including some very popular ones, that read the mouse directly via a serial port. These programs are only likely to operate properly if the mouse is a serial type connected to one of the standard serial ports. In fact some programs seem to insist on having a serial mouse connected to serial port 1 ("COM1").

Even with a printer and a serial mouse connected to the computer, the ports supplied as part of the standard system will almost certainly suffice. It is only if you need to add a second printer, a plotter, a modem, or some more exotic piece of equipment that further ports might be needed. You need to bear in mind that there is a limit to the number of serial and parallel ports that can be added to a PC. You can have up to three parallel ports ("LPT1" to "LPT3"), and up to four serial ports ("COM1" to "COM4"). Most software supports LPT1, LPT2, COM1, and COM2, but support for ports numbers beyond these is something less than universal. In fact some software, rather unhelpfully, seems reluctant to recognise anything beyond LPT1 and (possibly) COM1. Before adding any serial or parallel ports, particularly anything beyond LPT2 or COM2, you should first ensure that your software will be capable of exploiting them.

When buying parallel and serial port cards you need to ensure that the card will provide the particular port you require. Most cards of this type now have configuration switches or jumper blocks so that they can be set to act as at least port 1 or port 2, and possibly as port 3 or 4. There are still some cards though, that have the port number or numbers preset. This is most common with single parallel and serial port cards, where the port is often preset as port 1. With twin serial port cards you sometimes find that the port is preset at port 1, with some optional components providing a second port that acts as port 2. Sometimes it is possible to change a port from (say) LPT1 to LPT2, but only by cutting links on the board and soldering in some jumper leads. This is obviously not a very convenient way of handling things.

When expanding a system, what you will almost certainly need is a card to provide port 2 or beyond. Expansion cards that do not allow you to set the port number via configuration switches or jumper blocks are probably best avoided. Bear in mind though, that you might be able to reconfigure one of the existing ports to operate as port 2, so that the new port can operate as port 1. Where possible it is preferable to leave the existing ports operating under their original numbers, and to have any new ports as port 2, port 3, or whatever. If you start reconfiguring the system it is very easy to get confused. Make a note of the original switch/jumper settings on the port cards before doing any reconfiguring. If necessary, you can then easily put the system back at "square one" and start from the beginning.

With the proliferation of multi-function cards you may find that you have more ports than you need! This does not matter provided you do not end up in the situation where two cards are providing the same port. If this should happen, at best you will probably find that neither card will function properly. At worst, the computer's hardware or the port expansion cards could sustain damage (although it has to be admitted that this is highly unlikely). Consulting the manual for a multi-function card will usually reveal that a certain set of configuration switch/jumper block settings will disable the port in question. Failing that, you may be able to set it as a higher port number. You can then simply ignore it, with no risk of it interfering with any of the other hardware. It is then ready for immediate use should you require a further port at some later time.

Setting the configuration switches or jumper leads for serial and parallel port cards is generally straightforward. The only slight complication is that some cards seem to have separate switches/jumpers for setting the port address and the interrupt number. The following table shows the addresses and interrupt numbers for COM1, COM2, LPT1, and LPT2 (the addresses are in hexadecimal and are the base addresses). Note that ports above LPT2 and COM2 operate under an unofficial standard, and are not included in this table.

Port	Address	Interrupt
LPT1	378	IRQ7
LPT2	278	IRQ5
COM1	3F8	IRQ4
COM2	2F8	IRQ3

There are other types of input and output port that can be fitted to a PC, such as analogue types. These are only needed for specialist applications such as scientific and medical research. Being specialised items they do not operate under any true standards. Most hardware of this type is fitted into the part of the input/output map reserved for "prototype cards". The exact address range is sometimes adjustable so that more than one card of this type can be used in the computer. However, when purchasing this type of hardware you need to make detailed enquiries in order to ensure that it will fulfil your requirements. You need to be especially careful that it is compatible with any software you will wish to use with it, or that any information you need in order to exploit the interface with your own software is provided by the vendor.

Mice and Tablets

The subject of mice and digitisers was raised in the previous section, and some further information on this topic would be in order. Mice for the PC are now produced by a substantial number of manufacturers. Most programs that support a mouse offer compatibility with both the Microsoft and Mouse Systems mice.

Some programs provide support for other mice, such as the Genius and Logitech varieties. However, as most mice are compatible with the Microsoft and (or) Mouse Systems mice, virtually any PC compatible mouse is usable with practically any PC software that offers mouse support. It is only fair to point out that in my experience, and that of others I have consulted, some inexpensive mice are not quite the bargains they at first appear. Reliability is not always what it could be, and neither is their compatibility in some cases. I would recommend using either the genuine article, or one of the more popular compatible types, unless you can check out the mouse with your equipment and software (or a similar set up) before buying the unit.

There is an important difference between a Microsoft mouse and a Mouse Systems type. The former has two buttons while the latter has three. Some compatible mice have three buttons and can be used in Microsoft or Mouse Systems emulation modes. The Microsoft mouse is by far the most popular type at present, and this has led to many mice only being produced in two button versions that are Microsoft but not Mouse Systems compatible. As any PC program that has mouse support is virtually certain to operate with a Microsoft or compatible mouse, the lack of the third button and a Mouse Systems emulation may not seem to be a major drawback. For most users, this is probably perfectly true. However, some programs (especially CAD types) either require the third button, or (more usually) can make good use of it where it is available. Before choosing a mouse it is well worthwhile checking to see whether or not any of your applications programs require or can usefully exploit the third button.

Digitising tablets are absolute pointing devices, rather than relative types (like mice). In other words, whereas a mouse can only be used to indicate movement in a certain direction, a digitising tablet deals in definite screen positions. If you lift a mouse from its mat, move it to a new position, and then replace it on the mat, the on-screen pointer will not move. With a digitising tablet, if you raise the "pen" or puck from the tablet, and then move it, the on-screen pointer will not move. However, as soon as you lower the "pen" or puck down onto the tablet the pointer will immediately jump to the appropriate position on the screen.

Most software is no easier to use with a digitising tablet, and they offer no real advantages. As they are about ten times more expensive than a mouse, this has led to them being far less popular. Where a program does properly support a digitising tablet, it might be well worth-while paying the extra money for one. Some CAD programs only use part of the digitiser for controlling the on-screen pointer, with the rest being given over to menus that are used instead of on-screen menus. This leaves virtually the whole screen free to act as the drawing area. Usually a large number of menus can be accommodated by the digitising tablet, and user defined menus incorporating macros (a series of commands) can be used. This enables quite complex tasks to be performed with a minimum of effort, and is one of the most efficient ways of working.

A tablet is very useful for use with illustration programs etc. where it is sometimes necessary to trace existing artwork into the computer. The ability of a tablet to operate using a "pen", or "stylus" as it is more correctly termed, makes it more suitable for applications where free-hand drawing is involved. Most people, even after gaining much experience with a mouse, find it difficult to use for free-hand drawing. A stylus is much better for this type of thing, being very much like using an ordinary pen or pencil.

Most programs that can utilize a digitising tablet offer support for the Hewlett Packard MM1201, and perhaps one or two other digitisers from the same manufacturer. Support for other makes of digitising tablet seems to be a bit "thin on the ground". However, most digitising tablets seem to offer an MM1201 emulation mode (or an emulation of some other Hewlett Packard digitiser). Most tablets, including the popular Hewlett Packard types, offer mouse emulations. This enables them to be used with virtually any PC software that has mouse support. They will only work as relative devices though, like the mice they are emulating. This still makes them an attractive proposition for use with something like a paint program, where the stylus is much easier to use than a mouse. Provided the stylus is kept within the maximum operating distance from the tablet, there is no difference between absolute and relative operation.

Accelerators

The original PC accelerator boards were designed to make a PC or PC XT perform like an 80286 based AT computer. There are now additional types, such as units to make an XT perform like an 80386 based AT, or to make an 80286 based AT perform like a 80386 equipped AT. Boards of this type seem like an ideal type of upgrade where faster operation is required, but in reality they are not quite as perfect as you might think. Their most obvious drawback is their cost, which is often quite high. This is not surprising when you consider that they are virtually a complete computer with (typically) about 1 megabyte of on-board RAM. The motherboard of the computer is left largely unused, but the add-in board utilizes the display, power supply, ports, case and disk drives of the host machine. Trading in your existing computer for a higher specification type might be cheaper. Another (and increasingly popular) alternative is to fit a higher specification motherboard in the computer. Both of these options bring the advantage of giving the full performance offered by the microprocessor. Using an accelerator card results in the microprocessor operating at full speed, but the operation of the computer as a whole might be slowed down to some extent by less than optimum disk accesses etc.

If an accelerator board can be obtained at a suitably low price, it might represent a very worthwhile upgrade. However, you need to be careful as these cards are often fussy about the computers they will operate in. In most cases they are not simple expansion cards of the type that you simply plug into any available expansion slot. Usually the microprocessor has to be removed from the motherboard, and a cable from the accelerator card is then connected to the vacant socket. One problem with this is simply that it generally means that the accelerator board is only usable with PCs that utilize one particular type of microprocessor. If the board is intended for an XT or compatible having an 8088 or V20 microprocessor, and you have an XT compatible that is based on an 8086 or

V30, then that board will almost certainly be unusable in your computer.

Another problem is that the cable which connects to the microprocessor socket is often quite short. This is not due to the manufacturer skimping — a long cable would prevent the system from operating reliably. This means that the accelerator card may have to be fitted in a certain expansion slot in order to get the cable to reach the socket, and if the layout of your computer's motherboard is at all non-standard, the cable might not reach the socket regardless of which expansion slot the accelerator card is fitted into. A further complication is that some motherboards have the microprocessor soldered in place, so that there is no easy way of removing it. Before you obtain an accelerator card it is obviously essential to check its suitability for your particular make and model of computer.

Chapter 2

INCREASING MEMORY

With so many modern programs requiring large amounts of memory in order to work at their best, and an increasingly large percentage needing the full MS/DOS allocation of 640k RAM in order to work at all, memory expansion is almost certainly the most popular form of PC upgrade these days. This is a potentially confusing subject, since there are two types of memory that can be used with PCs and PC XTs, and three types that can be used with AT computers.

Memory Map

Memory that comes within the normal 640k MS/DOS allocation is usually termed "base memory". If you have any form of modern PC it is unlikely that you will need to expand the base memory, as most machines now seem to be supplied with the full 640k of RAM as standard. RAM, incidentally, stands for "random access memory", and is the form of memory used for storing application programs and data. The contents of the RAM in a PC is lost when the computer is switched off, and is, for all practical purposes, lost if the computer is reset (whether a hardware or software reset). ROM (read only memory) is used for programs that must not be lost when the computer is switched off, which in the case of a PC means its BIOS program. The 8088 series of microprocessors can address 1 megabyte (1024 kilobytes or 1024k) of memory, but in a PC only 640k of this is allocated to RAM for program and data storage. The rest is set aside for purposes such as the ROM BIOS and the video RAM. Figure 2.1 shows the memory map for a PC.

If a memory upgrade should prove to be necessary, there are two possible approaches to providing this type of upgrade. Either the memory can be fitted on the motherboard, or it can be fitted in the form of an ordinary

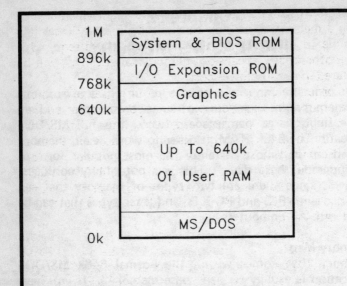

1M	System & BIOS ROM
896k	I/O Expansion ROM
768k	Graphics
640k	
	Up To 640k Of User RAM
	MS/DOS
0k	

Fig.2.1 Simplified PC memory map. In a practical system not all the graphics and (or) ROM area will be utilized.

expansion card. Not all motherboards can take the full 640k of RAM, although most modern boards can. Where both options are open to you, it is generally better to fit the memory on the motherboard. Apart from the fact that this avoids the cost of the expansion card, and you only need to buy the memory chips, it will also give faster operation. The computer usually puts in extra wait states when an expansion card is accessed, which means there are clock cycles where the operation of the microprocessor is suspended. This is to ensure that the computer does not work so fast that an expansion card can not keep up with it.

In the case of a memory board the wait states provide no useful function, since the memory board, if fitted with suitably fast memory chips, would have no difficulty in keeping pace with the rest of the computer. However, there is no way of eliminating the wait states when an expansion card is accessed. The only slight advantage of using a memory expansion card is that in many cases it is possible to use slower RAM chips than those required if the motherboard expansion method is used. This will be reflected in slightly lower cost.

In order to determine what type or types of memory chips are required for your particular computer, and where they fit on the motherboard, you must consult the manual. There is no standardisation of the memory chips on PC compatibles. There are four basic types of memory chip used in PCs, and these are the 4164, 41256, 41464, and 41000. These are all DRAM (dynamic random access) chips. There is another type of RAM (the static RAM), but these are not used in PCs.

The 4164 is not much used these days, since it provides only 64k of RAM. It provides only 1 bit by 64k of RAM, and eight chips are needed in order to provide 64k bytes of RAM. In fact PCs use a form of error checking on their RAM, called parity checking. This requires an extra bit of RAM, and therefore requires the use of nine 4164s per 64k of RAM. A few XT compatibles have the ability to switch off the parity checking, but it is normal to implement it and fit the extra RAM chips. Either way, making up the full 640k of base RAM using these chips would require an inordinate number of them. These days the most common use of 4164s is to make up 512k of RAM to the full 640k. This requires some 128k of RAM, or eighteen 4164s in other words.

41256 RAM chips are probably the most common type in PCs at present, although it seems likely that higher capacity chips will steadily usurp them over the next few years. They provide 256k by 1 bit of RAM, and for an XT there would normally be nine of these chips to provide 256k of RAM, or eighteen chips to provide 512k of memory. Early ATs have eighteen of these RAM chips to give 512k of memory, with no additional sockets to permit the full 640k of RAM to be installed on the motherboard. With these computers the extra 128k of RAM must be provided by an expansion card, and there are plenty of RAM boards designed to provide this filling out of the base RAM. More recent AT type PCs generally have provision for thirty-six 41256s on the motherboard, giving some 1 megabyte of RAM. Only 640k of this can be used directly by MS/DOS, but the other 384k can be used via RAM disk and disk cache programs. This is a subject we will pursue in some detail later in this chapter.

The 41464 chips provide 64k of RAM, but whereas the 4164 provides only 1 bit wide memory, the 41464s are 4 bit chips. This actually gives them exactly the same capacity as 41256s (4 x 64k = 256k), but the necessity for a parity bit, and nine rather than eight bit wide RAM, makes the 41464 less convenient for most PC RAM applications. However, some AT style motherboards can use this chip or the 41256. Quite a few modern XT compatible motherboards use four 41464s and two 4164s to make up the 512k provided by 41256 chips to the full 640k. This is some twelve less chips than are needed if this 128k of RAM is made up solely from 4164s, saving a lot of space on the motherboard (but not necessarily giving any great cost advantage).

With large amounts of memory being needed by many applications programs and operating systems such as OS/2, the 41000 memory chips are rapidly gaining in popularity. These provide 1024k (1 megabyte) by 1 bit of RAM. In order to equip an AT computer with 1 megabyte of RAM it therefore needs just nine of these chips. Only the more recent AT type motherboards are designed to take these memory chips, but where a motherboard can take them, they are almost certain to represent the cheapest method of providing the required amount of RAM. Of course, they will only provide 1 megabyte of RAM, or multiples of 1 megabyte, and on the face of it are of little use if you only require 512k or 640k of RAM. In practice, the cost might be only fractionally more than using 41256s to provide 512k of RAM, and will almost certainly cost less than using 41256s, 4164s and 41464s to provide 640k of RAM. For this reason it is not uncommon for AT compatibles to be fitted with 1 megabyte of 41000s as standard. Even if you have no immediate need for the extra RAM, there may be little or no cost advantage in having 512k or 640k instead!

Even some XT compatible motherboards are equipped to use these chips. Although the 8088 and 8086 microprocessors can not directly address the extra 384k of RAM, it is made accessible using a simple memory paging technique (similar in basic principle to the EMS type described later in this chapter). This can not be used directly by applications programs, but XT compatibles which have this extra RAM are normally supplied with software that enables it to be exploited as a RAM disk, a disk cache, or a printer spooler. Without any supporting software of this type, the extra 384k of RAM on an XT is of no use at all.

With standard AT compatibles and 80386 based AT machines it is now quite common for "interleaved" memory to be used. Looking at things in somewhat over-simplified terms, it consists of using each RAM chip to provide some of the memory over a large part of the memory range covered by the unit, rather than all the memory in one particular section of memory. Things can be arranged so that less stringent requirements are placed on the RAM's operating speed, enabling slower RAM chips to be used. This is helpful with the "turbo" 80286 based AT clones, and the faster 80386 AT type machines. Without the use of interleaving techniques these either require very fast and expensive RAM (possibly faster than any that is actually manufactured), or wait states have to be inserted in order to elongate memory accesses to the point where the RAM can keep up with the rest of the computer. Wait states are obviously undesirable, since they slow the computer down quite considerably. This largely or even totally negates the speed advantage of a higher clock rate.

Although memory interleaving might seem an ideal solution, it does have one drawback. This is simply that for a two way interleave there must be pairs of memory banks installed on the motherboard, or with a four way interleave there must be sets of four RAM chips. In other words, if you have a computer that can take up to four megabytes of RAM using 1 megabyte DRAM chips, and it has a two way interleave, either two sets or four sets of DRAM chips would have to be installed. You could therefore have two megabytes or four megabytes of RAM, but not one megabyte or three megabytes. Most modern AT compatible motherboards seem able to take 256k or 1M chips, and in our example above you would be able to have 512k or 1M of memory using 256k DRAM chips.

The speed ratings of SIMMs and DRAM chips are in nanoseconds (ns). A nanosecond is simply a thousand millionth of a second, and the speed rating is the time needed for the device to produce valid data (or read it) after it has been activated. Consequently, an 80 ns DRAM chip, for example, is faster than a 100 ns type, and could be used where 100 ns RAM is needed. 100 ns DRAM chips could not be guaranteed to operate reliably in a computer that required 80 ns DRAM chips.

Note that the integrated circuit type numbers given here are the basic ones. The actual type number marked on a chip usually has a suffix and a prefix. The prefix indicates the particular manufacturer of the chip, while the suffix usually just indicates the type of encapsulation. Memory chips are normally sold under their basic type numbers, rather than under a particular manufacturer's part number. The only type normally sold by electronic component retailers and PC upgrade specialists are the plastic d.i.l. (dual in-line) chips, which are the ones needed for normal PC motherboards and memory expansion cards.

SIMMs

There is a definite trend towards the use of SIMMs (single in-line memory modules) in modern PCs, particularly the 80286 and 80386 based machines. A memory module of this type is a small printed circuit board which is fitted with nine miniature DRAM chips of the surface-mount variety. This plugs into a socket on the motherboard, and this setup is like a sort of miniature version of the standard expansion slot system. Note that some SIMMs have only eight DRAM chips, and are not intended for use in PCs. As far as I am aware, the type that uses nine chips per module is the only type currently used in PCs. These modules come in 256k and 1 megabyte varieties, reflecting the type of DRAM chip they use. They are also available in a variety of speed ratings, again reflecting the type of DRAM chip they utilize.

Until recently these SIMMs were only used on AT type computers for expanding the memory well beyond the 640k DOS limit. A typical arrangement would be to have ordinary DRAMs on the motherboard to provide up to one or four megabytes of RAM, depending on the particular DRAM chips used, with provision for up to four one megabyte SIMMs to take the total amount of memory up to a maximum of eight megabytes. There is now a trend towards only using SIMMs for the computer's memory, especially with the 80386 and 80386SX based computers. At one time SIMMs were a very expensive way of buying RAM, but these days there seems to be little difference between DRAM chips and SIMMs offering the same amount of storage and the same speed rating. Any marginally higher cost in the memory is probably offset by savings in the production cost of motherboards that utilize SIMMs.

There seems to be a new development in the form of computers that have motherboards which do not take either DRAM chips or SIMMs directly. Instead they have special plug-in memory cards, which in turn take either DRAMs and (or) SIMMs. I am not quite sure what advantages (if any) that this system brings. As yet it seems to be used on relatively few computers. Note that the memory board slots on computers of this type are not standard memory expansion cards, but seem to be one-offs designed specifically for each computer. Unlike adding memory via ordinary expansion slots, no additional wait states are introduced when using these add-in memory cards, or when using SIMMs fitted directly onto the motherboard.

Expanded Memory and Caching

If you need to go beyond the 640k MS/DOS RAM limit, and this is only possible if your applications programs support some form of boosted memory, there are two basic options. The first of these is extended memory, which is only available if you have an AT machine, which can be 80286, 80386, or 80386SX based. This form of memory uses the microprocessor in a mode which is different to the one normally used for MS/DOS applications. Consequently, this RAM can not be used directly by MS/DOS applications programs. It addresses the extra RAM using additional pins of the microprocessor. These are simply not there on the 8088 and 8086 microprocessors, making this type of memory inapplicable to PC and PC XT type computers.

Although this memory can not be used directly by MS/DOS applications, it can be used to good effect in many instances. In a few cases the applications program may include the ability to store data in extended memory. In order to access this data the program will temporarily switch to the mode that gives access to the extended memory, copy the data into a section of the basic 640k of RAM where it can be accessed, and then switch back to the normal MS/DOS mode of operation again. This is a rather roundabout way of handling things, but it can be much quicker than the alternative of accessing data stored on a hard disk. This is especially so with 80386 based computers, which can change operating modes faster and more easily than 80286 based computers.

Another method of utilizing extended memory is to allocate some or all of it to a RAM disk. This is done using the device driver (usually RAMDRIVE.SYS) provided with all recent versions of MS/DOS. If your computer has (say) floppy disks A and B, plus hard disk C, then the RAM disk will be drive D. It can be used much like an ordinary disk drive, but it is essential to bear in mind that its contents will be lost when the computer is switched off. Any vital data stored in a RAM disk must therefore be saved onto the hard disk and (or) a floppy disk prior to turning off the computer, or it will be lost.

There are two basic (and similar) ways in which a RAM disk can be used to speed up programs. Programs that produce large amounts of data often have the ability to store some of the data on a disk drive once there is too much data to store in ordinary DOS RAM. This prevents the size of drawings, spreadsheets, or whatever, from being severely limited by the 640k MS/DOS RAM limit. On the other hand, it tends to slow things down quite dramatically, particularly if the disk drive used is a floppy type or a hard disk that does not have a particularly fast access time. Using a RAM disk as the temporary data store, or for any temporary files that the program may generate, can substantially speed up many programs.

A more sophisticated version of this technique can often be implemented when an applications program makes use of program overlays. This is where the program is too large to be accommodated by the 640k MS/DOS RAM. The standard way around this problem is to use program overlays, which means loading the main program into RAM initially, with the program then calling up routines from disk as and when necessary. This usually works on the basis of commands being loaded into memory, and being left there if they are used frequently, or soon overwritten by the program overlays for other commands if they are not used very often. This keeps the reading of overlays from disk to a minimum, which is an important factor if the overlays are large and the hard disk is not a fast type.

The overlays can be loaded into a RAM disk provided it has sufficient capacity. Many programs that use overlays enable the user to specify the drive where they are to be found. There is no point in loading overlays into a RAM disk unless the program can be made to read them from this source rather than the hard disk. In some cases it is possible to specify a drive where the program must look first for overlays. If it fails to find an overlay there, it will then look on the default drive/directory. This system has the advantage that you do not need to load all the overlays into RAM disk. If the RAM disk only has sufficient capacity to accommodate half of them, then you load the most often needed of the overlays into the RAM disk. These will be read from the RAM disk, while the others will be read from the hard disk in the usual way. At the other extreme, with a large RAM disk it might be possible to load the entire program into the RAM disk, complete with any support files, and run the program from there.

This method of using a RAM disk is not as good as having the entire program in the main memory and ready to operate instantly. Even using a RAM disk to hold program overlays, there might be a noticeable delay while large overlays are transferred to main RAM and then actually run. However, a RAM disk at least keeps any delays as short as possible.

A disk cache has similarities to a RAM disk used in the ways described previously. The basic action of a disk cache program is to monitor hard disk accesses. Some disk cache programs will also monitor floppy disk accesses, or can optionally be made to do so. However, in most cases it is only hard disk activity that is of significance when using a program of this type. When data, a program overlay, or whatever is read from the hard disk, the cache program stores it in extended memory. If that file is needed again, rather than loading it from the hard disk it is loaded from extended memory.

Depending on the size and number of files that are read from disk, and the amount of RAM allocated to the disk cache, it might be necessary for the cache to overwrite old files with new ones. This is generally organised on the basis of having a hierarchy, with the files that are needed more frequently taking precedence over those that are called-up infrequently. This clearly optimises use of the cache, with as few disk accesses as possible being made.

Of course, if enough memory can be allocated to the disk cache, it will be unnecessary for any file to be read from disk more than once during each session that the computer is used. A disk cache as small as 64k can apparently give a worthwhile improvement in speed with many programs. However, in general, the larger the disk cache, the more effective it is likely to be. Most disk cache programs can utilize base memory as well as extended memory. The problem with using base memory is that many applications programs now require all, or practically all the base memory, leaving too little base RAM for a really worthwhile disk cache.

The cache technique is in some ways less efficient than using a RAM disk in the ways described previously. It avoids the initial delay while everything that must be transferred to extended memory is duly loaded, but only at the expense of a short delay each time a file is loaded while the program is up and running. Also, a disk cache could waste time loading into extended memory files that will not be called-up again. The main attraction of a disk cache is that it is "transparent" to the user. You simply have the cache program run automatically from the CONFIG.SYS or AUTOEXEC.BAT file (as appropriate) at boot-up, and it will then get on with the job without you having to do anything further. Any program that you run which could benefit from a disk cache will automatically do so.

You will sometimes find programs that you thought would not benefit from a disk cache being speeded up quite significantly in some respects. For example, I use a large disk cache to speed up graphics programs and did not expect my word processor program to benefit from it. To a large extent it does not, but the spelling checker, after initially operating much as normal, then suddenly runs through long documents much faster than normal.

Expanded Memory

Having some extended memory fitted to your PC is certainly a great asset, but as pointed out previously, this type of memory can not be implemented on 8088 and 8086 based PCs. There is an alternative method of obtaining more memory though, and this method is usable with any PC. This type of memory is called "expanded" memory. It is often referred to as EMS (expanded memory system) or LIM (Lotus — Intel — Microsoft) memory. This second name is derived from the fact that these three large software houses got together to standardise this form of expanded memory. Most expanded memory these days conforms to the LIM 4.0 standard, but there are still plenty of expanded memory boards in use which conform to its predecessor, LIM 3.2. Many current expanded memory boards seem to be supplied with two device drivers so that they can operate under either standard. Here we will concentrate on the LIM 4.0 standard, as this is the version that new users of expanded memory are almost certain to utilize.

LIM 4.0 permits up to 32 megabytes of extra memory to be fitted to any true PC or compatible. Obviously this much RAM can not be accommodated by the 1 megabyte address range of the PC without resorting to some trickery. The method used is the well established one of page switched memory. This works on the basis of having a 16k block of memory, plus an output port. The 16k block is used when accessing any of the expanded memory. The output port is used to control the hardware via which the desired 16k block of memory is selected. Page switching techniques are not particularly efficient, since a certain amount of time is taken up in switching from one 16k block to another. On the other hand, extended memory on an AT involves switching backwards and forwards between two operating modes, which is not particularly fast either. The manuals for disk cache programs that can operate with extended or expanded memory generally recommend the use of the latter where a memory card board can be set to provide either type of memory.

Although simple enough in basic theory, there is a problem with a page switching memory system such as LIM 4.0 in that there is nowhere in the memory map for its 16k block of RAM and other addresses. The situation is made more difficult by the fact that a 64k block of address space is needed, because up to four 16k blocks can be available at any one time. All the addresses in the

PC memory map have official allocations. In practice though, no PC is likely to have the memory map filled with RAM or ROM at every address. The full 640k of RAM will often be present, plus the BIOS ROMs at the top of the map, and display RAM above the 640k of base RAM. This leaves a significant area between the display RAM and the ROM BIOS which is usually little used, and it is in a 64k block of addresses here that EMS page frame is located.

An important part of an EMS memory system is the driver program to accompany it. I believe that the more recent versions of DOS come complete with a suitable EMS 4.0 driver, but it is not included in earlier versions (including the much used MS/DOS versions 3.2 and 3.3). Most EMS cards are supplied complete with a suitable driver program, and they would seem to be of little use if they are not supplied with a suitable driver, and one is not included as part of your computer's operating system. In the driver program you can specify which output port address the board will use to select its pages of RAM.

There are two reasons for enabling the user to select the output port address. One is that the default address might already be used by another device. The other is that it is possible to use more than one EMS 4.0 memory card. If you are using (say) three memory boards, each fitted with 2 megabytes of RAM in order to obtain 6 megabytes of EMS memory, then each board must be set for a different output port address, and all three addresses would have to be specified when running the EMS driver program. The driver program does more than simply allocate output port addresses, and it includes routines that help applications programs to fully exploit the EMS memory. EMS memory is not restricted to use as a RAM disk or for disk caching. Some applications programs are designed to make direct use of it, and it seems to be better supported in this respect than extended memory. This is perhaps not surprising, since EMS memory is applicable to all PCs, not just AT type PCs, and it therefore has what is potentially a much larger user base.

This is admittedly a somewhat over-simplified explanation of EMS memory, but you do not really need to understand all the intricacies of the system in order to use EMS memory boards successfully. A major difficulty when installing virtually any memory expansion board is that there are often two or more banks of eight DIP switches which must be set up correctly. Fortunately, these days most boards are supplied together with a setup program. You run this program, answer questions about the start address, output port address, and amount of RAM fitted to the board. It then displays a diagram showing the correct settings for the DIP switches. In most cases, the line needed in the CONFIG.SYS file to run the EMS driver will also be shown, where applicable.

Until recently, PCs having on-board extended memory were quite common, but built-in support for EMS memory was unheard of. This seems to be changing, and some computers do now have the option of configuring memory above the 640k DOS limit as either extended or expanded memory. In some cases this is a proper hardware implementation of EMS. In a few cases though, the memory is of the extended variety, with software being used to provide an emulation of EMS. This method of software emulation using extended memory can be quite successful. However, be aware that in some cases the emulation might not be accurate enough. Also, especially with 80286 based computers, for some purposes (such as disk caches) an EMS emulation might be too slow to be worthwhile.

Choosing Extra RAM

If you need to increase the base RAM of your PC, or to increase the amount of extended memory, then it will almost certainly be better to opt for adding RAM chips or SIMMs to the motherboard, where this option is available. For an old PC which can only take up to 256k on the motherboard, there are 384k RAM boards available that will take the base RAM up to the full 640k. There are also 128k RAM boards available for ATs that can only take up to 512k on the motherboard. Many AT extended memory cards can provide so-called "back-fill" RAM. In other words, they can have the start address at 512k so that they provide 128k of base RAM, plus some extended RAM.

It might be possible to provide EMS RAM via on-board expansion, but unless you have a fairly modern AT compatible PC, it is unlikely that this option will be available to you. There are plenty of EMS memory boards available. The 16 bit cards are only intended for use in AT style PCs, and are not suitable for use in 8088 and 8086 based PCs. However, you can normally use 8 bit EMS boards in AT compatibles. If you have an AT it is a good idea to leave your options open by purchasing one of the many boards that can provide expanded or extended memory. Some can even be set to split their RAM between the two types of memory.

If you have some applications that require extended memory, and some that require expanded memory, you are unlikely to find a satisfactory way of switching a block of RAM between one type and the other. You will almost certainly have to fit both types of expansion. Also bear in mind that any memory allocated to a RAM disk or a disk cache will not be available to programs that can directly utilize expanded or extended memory. You must have sufficient memory available to accommodate all the programs that will wish to make use of it. With memory chip prices having fallen back from their high levels of the recent past, equipping a PC with large amounts of memory is not as expensive as it once was.

An important point to watch when fitting expanded RAM is that you have the necessary driver program. If your version of DOS does not include one, then you must obtain a board that comes complete with a suitable driver. An EMS card is unusable without this all-important driver program. If the driver is not run at switch-on, any applications program that can utilize EMS memory will simply ignore your EMS card, since it will have no way of knowing it is there, and will not have the support routines needed to utilize it.

Bear in mind that although the prices of many memory cards seem to be quite cheap, this is because they are often sold without any RAM chips fitted. Any supplier of RAM cards is almost certain to be able to supply boards with the required amount of memory already installed. In most cases it is significantly cheaper to buy the RAM chips from a specialist supplier and fit them yourself. When buying RAM chips or SIMMs, always read the instruction manual for your computer or memory card very carefully to make sure you obtain components of the right type and speed rating. Read the notes on fitting a maths co-processor that are provided in Chapter 1. Much of this information applies equally well to fitting DRAM chips.

Chapter 3
DISK DRIVES

For a stand-alone PC at least one disk drive is an essential feature. While there must be many thousands of single drive PCs in use and performing well, the complexity of much software these days is sufficient to warrant a second floppy disk drive, and (or) a hard disk drive. Fitting a second floppy disk drive to a PC is not a particularly complex task, and in most cases is very straightforward indeed. A hard disk is a somewhat more difficult prospect, and the hardware needed is slightly different depending on whether or not your PC is an AT type. Either way it is a task that should not be beyond any reasonably competent DIY enthusiast.

Floppy Drives

There are currently four types of floppy disk drive in common use with PCs. These are listed below. All four types use both sides of the disk incidentally.

> 3.5 inch, 80 track, 720k capacity
> 3.5 inch, 80 track, 1.44M capacity
> 5.25 inch, 40 track, 360k capacity
> 5.25 inch, 80 track, 1.2M capacity

The data on a floppy disk is stored magnetically on the metal oxide coating. This is much the same as the way in which an audio signal is recorded onto the tape in an ordinary compact cassette. In the case of a floppy disk though, the data is recorded onto a number of concentric tracks, or "cylinders" as they are sometimes termed. Each track is divided into a number of sectors, and there are nine sectors per track for a 5.25 inch 360k disk for example.

Originally the 5.25 inch 360k drives were used on PCs, PC XTs, and compatibles, while the 5.25 inch 1.2M type were used on ATs and compatibles. 3.5 inch drives have now been adopted as the industry standard, and in due course the 3.5 inch 720k and 1.44M drives should take over from the 5.25 inch 360k and 1.2M types respectively. Virtually all software is now either supplied on both sizes of disk, or is optionally available on 3.5 inch disks. The changeover is likely to be a gradual process though, since there is understandably a certain amount of consumer resistance. Like many PC users, I have accumulated a few hundred pounds worth of 5.25 inch disks of both the 360k and 1.2M varieties over the years, and am somewhat reluctant to simply abandon these in favour of 3.5 inch disks. Apart from the cost of the 5.25 inch disks that would have to be discarded, there is also the time taken to transfer everything to 3.5 inch disks to consider. It seems likely that the two sizes of disk will be used side-by-side for some time to come.

There is quite good compatibility between the two 5.25 inch disk formats. It is something less than perfect though. A 1.2M disk can not be read by a 360k drive, and it would be unreasonable to expect it to do so. Apart from the higher data density used by 1.2M drives, they also use twice as many tracks. With its wider record/playback head and only 40 head positions, a 360k drive will read two tracks at once when fed with 1.2M format disk. A 1.2M drive can read 360k disks, and in my experience there are not usually any reliability problems when doing this. A 1.2M drive can produce 360k drives, but there is a potential problem if this is done. What the drive actually does is to miss out every other track, so that it only uses 40 tracks per side of the disk. This is not quite the same as a genuine 40 track disk, in that the 80 track drive is effectively using only about half the width of each of the 40 tracks. When read using a real 40 track drive this can, and often does, produce problems.

If you start with an unused disk, the half tracks on which nothing is recorded will produce noise, but the disk drive may well be able to read the data through this increased noise. On the other hand, it might not! If the disk has ever been used in a real 40 track drive, and there has been data recorded across the full track width at some time, the chances of being able to read the data off the disk is negligible. The problem is that the original data on the disk is recorded across the full track width, but the 1.2M disk drive will only overwrite about half of each track. A 360k drive will therefore read back both sets of data simultaneously, giving a totally scrambled output. Paradoxically, another 1.2M drive will only read the half of the track which contains the wanted data, and will probably read a 360k disk of this type successfully, whereas a 360k drive will be unable to do so.

Compatibility between the two types of 3.5 inch disk is much better. The 720k drives can not read 1.44M disks, since they can not handle the higher data density. However, as both types of disk use 80 tracks, there are no problems if a 1.44M drive is used to produce 720k disks. They should be perfectly readable on both 1.44M and 720k drives.

Extra Drives

If you have a single floppy PC, it is likely that at some stage you will wish to add a second drive. Much of today's PC software requires at least a twin floppy computer, and it also makes life easier when backing-up disks, copying individual files from one disk to another, etc. Most hard disk PCs are supplied with only a single floppy as standard, and the hard disk might seem to render a second floppy drive superfluous. However, disk copying etc. is still much easier with the aid of a second floppy disk.

Another reason for adding a second disk drive, and one which applies equally to a single floppy computer, is to provide compatibility with both 3.5 inch and 5.25 inch disks. This is very worthwhile, even if only the lower density formats are supported. Most software is distributed on the lower capacity disks, and if data is being swopped between computers via floppy disks there will probably be no difficulty in using the lower capacity disks for this purpose.

The first point to bear in mind when adding a disk drive to a PC is that it must be of a type that is supported by the BIOS. Also, it must be a type that the computer's floppy disk controller can handle. There should be no difficulty when adding a 360k or 720k drive. Any standard floppy disk controller should be able to handle these properly, and virtually any BIOS will support either type. The only exception to this I have encountered is a modern AT BIOS which does not support the 360k format. Presumably this format is now considered obsolete, but adding a 360k drive to an AT is a popular upgrade, since a lot of people need to find a way around the slight 1.2M/360k drive incompatibility problem mentioned previously. If the setup program for your AT compatible computer does not offer the option of a 360k drive, then it may not be possible to use one with it successfully.

Older ROM BIOS chips do not support 1.44M 3.5 inch disk drives, and neither do older floppy disk controllers. These problems are not insurmountable, and fitting a more modern controller and set of ROM BIOS chips should enable a 1.44M drive to be fitted. Whether or not it is worth the effort is something you have to decide for yourself. Bear in mind that a change of BIOS can bring some unwanted side effects. You might find that some keys on the keyboard do not provide the right characters or are ignored completely, and that turbo/normal speed switching via the keyboard does not work. Finding a modern AT BIOS that is completely compatible with an older one can be difficult.

I have encountered problems when adding a 360k drive to an AT compatible having an old BIOS from one of the lesser known BIOS manufacturers. Everything worked fine as far as saving and loading data was concerned, albeit with rather slow access times. The problem was in formatting a 360k disk. The default format did not seem to be correct, and adding the appropriate DOS parameters to the format command simply resulted in messages along the line of "This Format Not Supported By Drive". The only way around the problem was to copy a blank but formatted

360k disk to the unformatted disk. This gave the "For-matting While Copying" message, and the disk was correctly formatted!

Trying to add a 1.44M or 1.2M disk drive to a PC or PC XT compatible is more than a little dubious. The floppy controllers in these computers are often unable to support either or both of these drive types. Even if the controller can cope, there can still be problems at the BIOS level. My advice is not to bother unless you are sure that the hardware and firmware can cope with a high density drive of the type you intend to fit.

There are two basic tasks to complete when fitting a floppy disk drive. The first is to get it physically fixed in place, and the second is to get it connected to the controller correctly. For PC and XT compatible com-puters the disk drives normally bolt directly to the dirve bay. The exact methods of fixing depend on the type of case used on the computer, and you may have a choice of fitting screws into the sides of the drives, into the base panel, or both. Usually the method of fixing will be the same as for the existing disk drive, and can be ascertained by looking to see how this drive is fixed in place.

If you are lucky, your computer will have been supplied with some additional drive fixing screws and one or two other odds and ends of hardware. Alternatively, disk drives are sometimes supplied complete with a set of four fixing screws. If not, it could be difficult to locate a source of suitable screws. It is important these screws are quite short. Otherwise there is a risk of them pene-trating too far into the drive and causing damage. Provided you have the correct fixing screws, fixing a drive into this type of computer is unlikely to give any real difficulties.

Standard AT style cases use a somewhat different method of drive fixing. Two plastic rails are used, and are bolted one per side onto the drive. The slightly pointed end of the rails should be towards the rear of the drive. This assembly is then slid into place in one of the drive bays, pushing it right back as far as it will go. A couple of metal clips are then bolted in place at the front of the bay. These press hard against the plastic mounting rails, and hold the drive assembly firmly in place. Once again, if you look at the existing disk drive, you will see from this how it is fixed in place.

The guide rails are almost totally standardised, but I have encountered one or two AT compatibles which seem to use a non-standard type of rail. If your computer falls into this category, and it was not supplied complete with an extra set of guide rails, adding an extra disk drive could be problematic. Possibly your dealer will be able to supply a set of suitable rails. Alternatively, you will have to improvise a bit with a standard set of rails, or make up some rails yourself from some scraps of plastic. If your computer does use the standard type, it is quite likely that it will have been supplied together with an extra set. It is also possible to buy disk drives complete with AT mountings. A dealer specialising in PC accessories should be able to supply them in the event that you did not obtain a set with either your computer or the drive.

Connections

Connection from the floppy controller card to the disk drive is via a standard cable. In most cases you will find that the necessary connector for a second disk drive is already present on the disk drive lead fitted in your computer. If this is the case, simply plugging it onto the drive is all you need to do. The plug should be polarised, so that it can not be fitted the wrong way round. The necessary "key" (just a small metal rod) on each of the drive lead connectors are sometimes missing. You should find that the connector numbers, or some of them, are marked onto the connector on the disk drive. They might also be marked on the drive lead connectors, and a coloured lead (as opposed to the grey of all the others) on the cable itself should denote the pin 1 end of the lead/connector. Pin 1 on the drive lead connector couples to pin 1 on the drive's connector.

72

You must also connect the power supply to the disk drive. Modern PC power supplies seem to have about four or five leads and connectors for disk drives. Simply connect the plug on any spare lead to the power socket on the disk drive. This is a properly polarised plug, and it is impossible to connect it to the drive around the wrong way. With old PCs there may not be a spare disk drive power cable. You will then need to obtain an adaptor which takes one of the drive power leads and splits it to permit connection to two drives.

There is a potential problem with 3.5 inch drives in that they mostly use a miniature version of the standard disk drive power socket. However, 3.5 inch drives intended for use in PCs are normally supplied in a chassis which includes an adaptor that enables the drive to be connected to a standard (full size) disk drive connector. You need to be slightly careful when ordering a 3.5 inch drive for use in a PC. At one time PC cases only had drive bays for 5.25 inch drives. All 3.5 inch PC drives were therefore fitted in chassis which enabled them to be mounted in 5.25 inch drive bays, as well as making the conversion to the standard size power connector, as mentioned previously. Some modern PC cases, especially the compact and tower varieties, include 3.5 inch drive bays. These will not accommodate a drive which is fitted into a 5.25 inch chassis. You therefore need a drive complete with 5.25 inch chassis if it is to be fitted into a standard PC drive bay, or without this chassis if it is to be fitted into a 3.5 inch bay. Most suppliers seem to sell the chassis separately, so you do not need to buy it if you have 3.5 inch bays in your computer.

Floppy Cables
The standard PC floppy disk drive cable consists of a length of 34 way ribbon cable which is fitted with a 34 way IDC (insulation displacement connector) edge connector at the floppy drive end. The connector at the controller end is not totally standardised, but most controllers require a 34 way IDC connector, or a 34 way IDC edge

connector. Most cables are for twin drives, and have an extra 34 way IDC edge connector fitted about 150 millimetres or so down the cable from the other floppy drive connector. In a standard floppy drive setup, the two connectors would be wired in exactly the same way. Pin 1 at the controller would connect to pin 1 of both drive connectors, pin 2 would connect to both of the pin 2s, and so on. The two drives do not operate in unison, and both try to operate as drive A, because there are jumper leads on the drives which are set to make one operate as drive A, and the other as drive B. These jumper blocks are normally a set of four pairs of terminals marked something like "DS0", "DS1", "DS2", and "DS3" (or possibly something like "DS1" to "DS4"). The instruction manual for the disk drive (in the unlikely event of you being able to obtain it) will make it clear which of the many jumper blocks are the ones for drive selection. Drive A has the jumper lead on "DS0", while drive B has it on "DS1".

Things could actually be set up in this fashion in a PC, but it is not the standard way of doing things. Instead, both drives are set as drive B by having the jumper lead placed on "DS1". The so-called "twist" in the cable between the two drive connectors then reverses some of the connections to one drive, making it operate as drive B.

This may seem to be an unusual way of doing things, but there is apparently a good reason for it. If you obtain a PC disk drive, whether for use as a replacement for a worn out drive A, or as a newly added drive B, the same drive configured in exactly the same way will do the job. This avoids the need for dealers to stock two different types of drive, that in reality are the same type of drive but configured slightly differently. For the DIY PC upgrader it makes life easier in that any drive sold for use in a PC should work perfectly without the need to alter any of the configuration jumpers. Of course, if you buy a drive that is not specifically for use in a PC, bearing in mind that the 360k and 720k drives are used in other computers, it might not be set up correctly for operation in a PC. The elusive instruction booklet for the disk drive is then more than a little useful.

If you decide to make your own floppy drive cable, you need about 0.5 metres of 34 way IDC ribbon cable. This is available in grey plus one coloured lead, or with the leads in ten or more different colours. The multi-coloured type is generally easier to use, but as it is significantly more expensive it is less popular. It is slightly better in the current context, but the grey variety should suffice.

The controller end of the cable must have a 34 way IDC connector if the controller plug is of the type having two rows of gold coloured prongs sticking up on the board. If the controller has an edge connector (i.e. 17 strips of copper on each side of a protruding part of the circuit board) then a 2 by 17 way 0.1 inch pitch IDC edge connector is required. This is the type of connector that is always needed at the disk drive end of the cable, and for a twin drive cable you will need two of them. In theory, there is no difficulty in placing the end of the cable into the slot for it, and forcing the rear cover of the connector down onto the cable. This forces the cable down onto the forked terminals, which cut through the insulation and into the wires. This gives good, reliable connections between the connectors and the wires in the cable. The rear of the connector will then snap into place and lock there, holding the cable firmly in place.

In practice it is not always as easy as this. The ease or difficulty with which the cable can be fitted depends to some extent on the particular cable and connectors used. Sometimes the cable fits perfectly into position, and little effort is needed to push it down onto the terminals. In most cases though, the cable needs to be very carefully positioned, or the terminals may not align properly with the wires. This can result in some terminals being left unconnected, or can even result in a terminal connecting two wires and short circuiting them. A substantial amount of pressure may be needed in order to push the rear section down into the locking position, and a vice may well be needed in order to do this.

Assuming that the drives are to be set up in the standard

PC fashion (i.e. both set up as drive B), then the twist in the cable must be included. This means putting two lengthwise splits in the cable so that wires 10 to 16 (inclusive) are separated from the other wires. A single twist is then placed in these wires, and a band of adhesive tape about 25 millimetres from the end of the cable is used to hold the three pieces back in place so that an IDC connector can be fitted at the end of the cable. The second IDC edge connector is fitted about 150 millimetres from the end of the cable, but ahead of the twist in the cable. The connector at the end of the cable couples to drive A, while the other one connects to drive B. Figure 3.1 shows this general scheme of things.

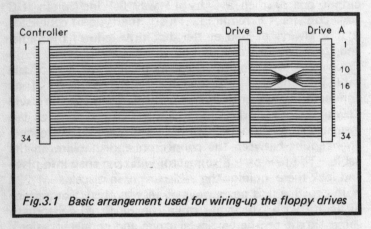

Fig.3.1 Basic arrangement used for wiring-up the floppy drives

The main point to watch when producing a do-it-yourself cable of this type is that there are no connectors fitted upside-down. In other words, make sure that pin 1 on the controller connects through to pin 1 on each of the disk drives, without any connectors fitted the wrong way round resulting in pin 1 connected to pin 34, pin 2 connected to pin 33, pin 3 connected to pin 32, and so on. If in any doubt about your ability to produce a suitable cable, then it is probably better to buy a ready-made one. As pointed out previously, when adding a second drive to a PC it is not normally necessary to change the drive cable, as the one supplied with the computer will almost certainly have a connector for a second drive. If it does not, but it does have the "twist" in the cable, then it may well be possible to add the second connector to it, rather than starting from scratch and producing a totally new cable.

Termination Resistors

Every disk drive has a set of eight termination resistors. These connect to certain inputs of the drive, and ties them to the +5 volt supply rail. They are what is termed "pull-up" resistors. However many disk drives are used, only one set of termination resistors should be present. It is only the drive at the end of the cable that should have these resistors. Therefore, if you fit a second drive to a PC, as it will fit mid-cable, it will not require its termination resistors.

These resistors are normally in the form of a single component, rather than eight individual resistors. They will be mounted in a socket of some kind, and this will often be of the standard 16 pin d.i.l. integrated circuit type. A socket of this type has two rows of eight terminals 0.3 inches apart. The resistor pack itself will probably be in the form of a black plastic component having two rows of eight pins. The resistors have a value of 220 ohms, and so the component will be marked something like "220R", plus some other characters in most cases. There is a trend for modern drives to use a s.i.l. (single in-line) resistor pack. These have nine pins in a single row, usually with 0.1 inch pin spacing. Like the d.i.l. resistor packs, they are mounted in a socket so that they can be easily removed. In fact the s.i.l. variety are generally more easily removed than the d.i.l. type. With any d.i.l. component it is a good idea to use a screwdriver to carefully prise it free from the socket. Keep the termination resistor pack safe somewhere in case it should be needed at some later time. In fact you should always keep anything removed from the computer when performing upgrades. You never know when these odds and ends will be needed again.

If you have any difficulty locating the termination resistor pack, the instruction manual for the disk drive should include a diagram that shows its position. In some drives the resistor pack is permanently wired in place, but it can be disconnected by removing a jumper lead. Again, the instruction manual for the disk drive should give details of which jumper lead to remove. If the resistor block is not removed, it is quite likely that the extra drive will still work perfectly, and will not hinder the operation of the original disk drive. However, it is obviously much more satisfactory if it can be located and removed, or disconnected via the appropriate jumped lead.

Hard Disks

A hard disk is very much like an ordinary floppy type, but in a highly refined form. The disk itself is a permanent part of the drive, and is not interchangeable like floppy disks (hence the alternative name of "fixed" disk). The disk is made of metal and is rigid (hence the "hard" disk name). The disk spins at a much higher rate that is about ten times faster than the rotation speed of a floppy disk. Furthermore, it rotates continuously, not just when data must be accessed. This is an important factor, since one of the main advantages of a hard disk is the speed with which data can be accessed. Having to wait for the disk to build-up speed and settle down at the right speed would slow down disk accesses by an unacceptable degree. In fact the high rotation speed would result in accesses to a hard disk actually being slower than those to a floppy disk. A slight drawback of this continuous rotation is that computers equipped with hard disks are notoriously noisy! The high rotation speed of the disk aids rapid data transfers. Data can typically be read from disk in less than a tenth of the time that a floppy disk would take to handle the same amount of data.

Although the disk of a hard disk is not changeable, it has a very high capacity so that it can accommodate large amounts of data and several large applications programs if necessary. This is achieved by having what is typically many hundreds of cylinders with (usually) some seventeen sectors per cylinder. The lowest common hard disk capacity is 10 megabytes, and these days 20 megabytes is the lowest capacity offered by most suppliers. Hard disks having capacities of about 40 to 60 megabytes are quite commonplace, and disks having capacities of over 100 megabytes are available. In most cases the "disk" is actually two, three, or four disks mounted one above the other on a common spindle. This enables around three to eight record/playback heads and sides of the disk to be used, giving higher capacities than could be handled using a single disk.

An important point that has to be made right from the start is that hard disks are highly intricate and quite delicate pieces of equipment. They must be treated with due respect, and protected from excessive jolts and vibration if they are to provide long and trouble-free service. The risks can be exaggerated. You are unlikely to damage a hard disk drive simply by picking up the computer in which it is fitted, and carrying it across to the other side of the room. On the other hand, dropping the computer could well result in serious damage to the hard disk drive. Hard disk units are hermetically sealed so that dust can not enter. This is crucial, due to the high rotation speed of the disk. Apparently, the heads are aerodynamic types which glide just above the surface of the disk, never actually coming into contact with it. If the two should come into contact, even via an intervening speck of dust, the result could easily be severe damage to the surface of the disk, and possibly to the head as well. Never open up a hard disk drive if you ever intend to use it again!

Interfaces
Adding a hard disk drive to a PC breaks down into three basic tasks. First it must be bolted in place inside the computer. Then it must be connected up to the power

supply and a suitable hard disk controller. Finally, it must be formatted and made ready for use with the MS/DOS operating system. Usually the operating system will be installed on the hard disk so that the computers boots-up from the hard disk at switch-on. As we shall see shortly, formatting and making a hard disk ready for use is a more complex business than formatting a floppy disk. Unless you have access to suitable software a hard disk that has been correctly fitted and installed physically will be of no practical value.

Physically installing a hard disk is much the same as installing a floppy disk. All PC floppy disk drives, with the possible exceptions of some very early types, are of the half height variety. The same is true for most hard disk drives, but some older and high capacity types are full height devices. In order to accommodate one of these you must have two spare drive bays, and they must be one above the other, not side-by-side. You will also need two sets of fixing screws, slide rails, or whatever. As there is no disk swopping with a hard disk drive, it does not need to be mounted in a drive bay that has an open front. On XT computers all the drive bays are normally of the open variety. This is done so that the drive light is visible, and you can see from this whether or not the drive is being accessed. This is helpful, but obviously not essential.

With the standard AT style case the left hand drive bays are enclosed, and the drive light of a hard disk installed in either of these will not be visible to the user. However, the drive light on a hard disk drive installed in an AT computer is switched on all the time the computer is switched on, so the user is not missing much! The hard disk controller includes an output for a drive indicator light, and the standard AT style case has a suitable indicator light fitted on the left hand section of the front panel.

When obtaining a hard disk drive and a controller card you need to be aware that there is more than one type of interface in common use. What must currently count as the nearest thing to a standard PC hard disk interface card is the ST412/ST506 type (or an equivalent type) using MFM (modified frequency modulation) signal encoding. Some of the more recent controller cards of this type use the alternative method of coding known as RLL (run length limited). This second method has the advantage of giving 50% greater capacity from the hard disk, plus the potential for faster data transfer rates.

This might seem too good to be true, and it probably is. Several hard disk manufacturers only seem to recommend this type of controller for use with drives that are tested to higher standards. There have been numerous reports of people who have used RLL controllers with ordinary hard disk drives, and who have suffered severe reliability problems before too long. I would certainly not recommend the use of an RLL controller with any hard disk drive which the manufacturer does not specifically state as suitable for use with this type of controller. There is a lot to be said in favour of obtaining the hard drive and controller as a pair, guaranteed by the retailer to be fully compatible. This avoids the risk of obtaining a hard disk and controller that have different interfaces, or a method of signal encoding that might give less than full compatibility. If any problems should arise, then the retailer will almost certainly be legally obliged to sort things out.

Connections from the controller to the hard disk drive are made via two ribbon cables with this type of interface. A 34 way type carries the control signals while a 20 way type carries the data signals. These are similar to a standard floppy disk drive cable, having IDC edge connectors at the drive ends of the cables, and IDC connectors at the controller end. Note that unlike the 34 way floppy drive cable, the 20 way hard disk cable does not incorporate the "twist". The 34 way type may do so, depending on the way in which the hard drive or drives are set up. Apparently, IBM computers invariably incorporate the twist, but this has been absent on all the XT and AT compatibles that I have encountered. Do not use a floppy drive cable as a 34 way hard disk cable. If the cable must incorporate the "twist", it should be on wires 25 to 29 inclusive, not wires 10 through 16 as on a standard floppy drive cable.

These cables are not too difficult to make up yourself, but they are readily available ready-made at quite low cost. They are often supplied with hard disk drives and controller cards. If two hard disk drives are used, they will require separate 20 way cables which connect to separate 20 pin connectors on the controller card. A single 34 way cable is used for twin drives, with floppy drive "daisy-chain" style interconnections being used. Incidentally, the power supply connector on a hard disk is normally of the same type as that used for floppy drives. Consequently, the cables and connectors of a PC power supply are fully compatible with the power input connector of a standard hard disk drive.

The SCSI (small computer systems interface) hard disks and controllers that were once a great rarity seem to be slowly gaining in popularity. As its name suggests, it is not actually a form of hard disk controller, but a general purpose computer interface. It has not been used very much with PCs in the past, as their open architecture, generous number of expansion slots, and tremendous popularity, has made SCSI rather superfluous in a PC context. However, there is now a great deal of SCSI oriented equipment available and in circulation, which has led to it making more impact on the PC world. While SCSI offers great scope for expansion, with the possibility of having numerous hard drives connected to a single computer, it still has its drawbacks as far as the average PC user is concerned. It is likely to be relatively expensive, there can be problems with a lack of absolute standardisation, and probably few users really require anything like the amount of expansion it offers. It is probably something that is best left to the more experienced PC upgraders at the present time.

The ESDI (enhanced small device interface) system is a specialised disk/tape drive interface that can handle very fast data transfers. In fact it can handle such high transfer rates that it is probably only a worthwhile proposition on higher performance PCs. For low to medium capacity drives the ST412/ST506 interface still seems to be by far the most popular, but for high capacity drives of about 70 megabytes or more the ESDI type seems to be establishing itself as the new standard.

There are one or two other PC disk drive interfaces in existence, but these would seem to be little used these days. The only alternative type which I have experienced first hand is the type used on some Xebec drives, where there is a single and large connecting cable between the drive and controller. It is probably best to avoid any of the lesser used types unless you can buy them as a complete package consisting of the drive, controller and connecting cable or cables. When obtaining any unusual PC peripherals you should try to ensure that spare parts and service will be available for a reasonable period of time.

The standard method of interconnection for PC hard drives and their controllers has already been covered. Bear in mind that, like floppy drives, hard disk drives normally have a set of termination resistors. In a twin hard drive setup only the resistors on the drive at the end of the 34 way control cable should be fitted. Also, like floppy drives, hard disk drives have drive number selectors. If a "twisted" cable is used, both drives should be set as drive 1. If a "straight" type is used, then they should be set as drives 0 and 1.

XT/AT Controllers

It is important to realise that the hard disk controllers for AT and XT computers are very different, and are quite definitely not interchangeable. The XT types are 8 bit cards which incorporate a ROM BIOS. The AT types are usually 16 bit cards and they utilize the ROM BIOS on the motherboard. Both types are available with or without built-in twin floppy drive controllers. For AT computers the use of combined floppy/hard disk controllers now seems to be the norm, and as a hard disk is virtually a standard item on AT type computers this would seem to be a sensible way of handling things. For the 8088 and 8086 based PCs a hard disk is a popular add-on, and the use of separate controllers seems to be the more common approach.

If we start with the setting up process using an XT style hard disk controller, the controller must know what type of hard disk it is controlling. With the early controller cards the options were rather limited, and you had to choose a disk from the very limited range supported by the controller card. Modern controllers are mostly much more flexible. Usually jumper blocks or configuration switches are used to select one of several popular hard drive types. There is usually an additional option which allows the user to specify the important drive parameters (numbers of heads, cylinders, etc.). This information is then stored on the disk itself, and read off by the system as and when necessary. This sounds a bit like lifting yourself up by your bootlaces, but it seems to work alright in practice!

A program in the controller's built-in ROM BIOS enables the drive parameters to be specified (if necessary), and what is termed a "low level format" to be carried out. Formatting of a floppy disk drive is done in a single process, with markers being placed on the disk to indicate the positions of the various tracks, and sectors, and the basic framework of the directory being laid down. The complexity of a hard disk has led to a two tier formatting process being used. These are the low level format mentioned above, and the so-called "high level" format. The low level format consists of laying down the tracks and sectors, and is much like floppy disk formatting, but it does not write a blank file allocation table or create a root directory. This is done by the high level format, which is done using the ordinary MS/DOS "FORMAT" command.

Obviously the first step is to set the jumpers or switches for the appropriate type of disk drive. The manual will list the drives that are supported, but probably not by manufacturer and type number. Instead, for each type there will be a list of parameters, such as the capacity, number of heads, number of cylinders, and the step rate. All this information should be shown on the performance report supplied with every drive, and might be marked on an information sheet on the drive itself. If your drive's specification does not match any of those listed, then you will need to select the mode that enables the user to specify the parameters.

Next the setup and low level formatting program must be run. The manual for the disk controller will inform you of the correct method of starting the setup/low level format program. This is usually achieved using the MS/DOS "DEBUG" command, and an instruction such as "DEBUG (RETURN) —G=C800:5 (RETURN)". However, the exact start up instruction varies slightly from one controller to another. Once the program is running you will almost certainly be presented with menus and questions to answer, and these programs are mostly straightforward to use.

Bad Sectors

If you select the "key-in" mode, you will have to specify certain parameters for your drive before the low level format can be started. You will also be given the option of mapping bad sectors on the disk. Virtually all hard disks have weak spots on the magnetic coatings of the disks, and these are sorted out when the manufacturer gives the disk its final testing. The bad sectors should be indicated on the test report sheet provided with the hard disk, and in most cases a label stuck on the drive itself also lists the bad sectors. It is just a matter of typing the appropriate head and cylinder numbers into the computer when prompted by the setup/format program. Obviously these bad sectors represent a loss of the drive's capacity, but in most cases they represent an insignificant loss of about 0.1%. Once the bad sectors have been indicated, the low level format can proceed. The program will probably report on its progress as it works its way through each head and cylinder. This process can take quite a while as there is likely to be a large number of tracks to format.

Having reached this stage it is time to exit the setup/low level format program and go back to the operating system. Before using the MS/DOS "FORMAT" program you must first prepare the disk using the "FDISK" command. This creates a DOS "partition", and in most cases the whole of the disk will be set as a single "partition". Note though, that MS/DOS versions earlier than version 4.0 do not permit the first DOS partition to be more than 32 megabytes. If you have a disk with a capacity of more than 32 megabytes, either it must be used as a 32 megabyte type, or it must be split into two partitions with the first one set at no more than 32 megabytes.

If two partitions are used, and assuming that the floppy drives are A and B, the primary partition of the hard disk will act as drive C, with the second partition operating as drive D. Some hard disks are supplied complete with partitioning software, but you may well prefer to use the MS/DOS "FDISK" command. However, if you have a version of MS/DOS earlier than version 3.3, it will not be able to provide two partitions. You will then need suitable partitioning software, or an upgrade to version 3.3 or 4.0 of MS/DOS. With version 4.0 of MS/DOS there is no necessity to opt for two partitions, since primary partitions of up to 2 gigabytes (two thousand megabytes) are acceptable. Of course, you might consider it to be more convenient to have the drive's capacity split into two sections, and this is, of course, fully supported by MS/DOS 4.0.

Having followed the prompts and completed the "FDISK" command (simply accepting the default options is all that is needed in most cases), the "FORMAT" command can then be run. Like a low level format, this might take several minutes to complete the task, since there are a large number of tracks to be processed and checked. Presumably the operating system will need to be placed onto the disk, and this can be accomplished during the high level formatting process by including the "/S" parameter in the format instruction (i.e. "FORMAT C: /S

(RETURN)"). If the disk is operating as drive C and drive D, they must both be formatted using separate "FOR-MAT" commands. Of course, the system should only be placed on disk C.

AT Hard Disks

Having the ROM BIOS for the hard disk system included on the motherboard is, on the face of it, a more advanced way of handling things. It does have a drawback though, in that this method, as implemented on an AT, does not allow for the use of the "key-in" method of telling the system the parameters of the hard disk drive. If the BIOS does not support your particular hard disk drive, then it can not be used with the computer. Actually this is not strictly correct, and there are ways around the problem. The most sophisticated method is to use a special kit to produce BIOS ROMS that can handle a drive of any specified parameters. This is a rather costly solution, and as the necessary kits do not seem to be available in the U.K., it is one that is probably of academic interest only.

The simpler solution is to choose the set of parameters that is the nearest match for your drive. When doing this you must be careful not to select a set of parameters that leads the system to believe that the drive has heads or tracks which it does not possess. In other words, you must select a number of heads and a number of cylinders that in both cases are equal to or less than the actual number of heads and cylinders that the drive possesses. This means losing a certain amount of the disk's capacity, but it will usually result in a loss of no more than a few percent.

As an example, I once had to use a hard disk having six heads and 853 cylinders as a six head 820 cylinder type. This represents a loss of capacity of under 4%, and as the drive was attractively priced, it still represented good value for money. Note though, that in some cases a much larger reduction in capacity might be necessary, and that what seems like a bargain drive might not represent very good value for money when used in many AT computers.

This list is for the standard fifteen drive types supported by the original AT BIOS. This is well standardised, and seems to be accurately copied by all AT clones. The capacity in megabytes is given to the nearest megabyte. "Precomp" is the write precompensation starting cylinder.

No.	Cylinder	Heads	Precomp	Megabytes
1	306	4	128	10
2	615	4	300	20
3	615	6	300	31
4	940	8	512	62
5	940	6	512	47
6	615	4	−1	20
7	462	8	256	31
8	733	5	−1	30
9	900	15	−1	112
10	820	3	−1	20
11	855	5	−1	35
12	855	7	−1	50
13	306	8	128	20
14	733	7	−1	43
15			Reserved	

Modern BIOSs seem to offer considerably more than the basic fifteen drive types. In fact most offer some forty-seven types, and a few offer substanially more than this. Unfortunately, there seems to be something less than total standardisation of drive types above type fifteen. There is no point in providing details of drive types above type fifteen here, since the data I would provide might not match up with the BIOS of the particular ATs you will be dealing with. If you have more than one AT, and they are from different manufacturers, you may well find that their BIOS drive tables are slightly different.

The documentation supplied with the computer may give details of the drive types supported by the BIOS. Alternatively, many BIOSs these days seem to incorporate a setup program, and if this is run you might be able to scroll through a list of drive types (this is sometimes accessed by calling up a help screen using the "F1" function key). Yet another alternative is the test and diagnostics program built into some BIOSs. This might provide a list of the supported drive types. If you have a computer fitted with an old BIOS you might find it necessary to fit a more modern one in order to use your selected hard disk drive.

It is important to realise that you can not use a hard disk drive with an AT style computer unless its BIOS supports that type of drive (or a very similar type), and the right drive type number has been entered into the CMOS RAM using the setup program. Normally the setup program is run and the appropriate drive type number is entered after the low level format has been carried out. Informing the system that the hard disk drive is present prior to this could result in the computer hanging-up. The setup program must be used prior to the high level format, or the operating system will fail to recognise the existence of the hard disk drive, and will refuse to format it.

The first step in setting up the hard disk drive is to perform a low level format. Whereas XT type hard disk controllers normally incorporate formatting software, this is not always present in AT BIOSs. In fact I have only encountered such a facility in an AMI BIOS, where it was included as part of the built-in test and diagnostics program. You may find that your computer was supplied with some utility programs, including a hard disk low level formatter. Software of this type is sometimes supplied with hard disk drives. These programs are often quite sophisticated, and if required, will perform both the low level and high level formatting. If you do not have a suitable formatting program, you must obtain one before you can proceed any further.

Having performed a low level format, you then run the setup program and enter the appropriate drive type number into the CMOS RAM. Then the MS/DOS "FDISK" and "FORMAT" commands are used, in exactly the same way that they are used when performing a high level format on a hard disk fitted in an XT computer.

Interleave Factor

Some low level formatting programs will ask you to enter the "interleave factor". You will not always be asked for this, since some formatter programs seem to select a sensible (but not necessarily optimum) value for the hardware in use. If in doubt you can usually just settle for a default value, or type in a likely value. Getting the value wrong will not stop the hard disk from working, but it could result in data transfer rates that are far slower than the maximum rate achievable by the system. This can be quite noticeable in use, particularly when large amounts of data are being moved around.

Interleave factors are not very difficult to understand. The hard disk reads data from a sector of the disk, and after a short delay while this is processed it goes on to read the next sector. The most obvious way of arranging

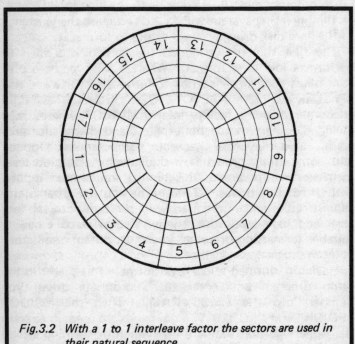

Fig.3.2   With a 1 to 1 interleave factor the sectors are used in their natural sequence

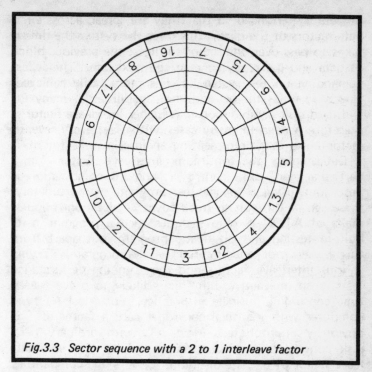

Fig.3.3 Sector sequence with a 2 to 1 interleave factor

data on the disk is in the manner shown in Figure 3.2, which is an interleave factor of 1. The problem with this is that by the time the first sector has been read and the data has been "digested" by the system, the head will probably have gone past the beginning of the next sector. This results in the disk having to do virtually a complete rotation before the head comes to the beginning of the next sector in the sequence, wasting a considerable amount of time (in disk access terms) in the process. It would be misleading to say that this will always happen, and some systems can operate very successfully with an interleave factor of 1. However, the only PCs that can achieve this are fast 80286 or 80386 based machines using special hard disk controllers.

The obvious solution to this problem is to use an interleave factor of 2, as in the example of Figure 3.3. Blocks of data are arranged so that they are spread across alternate sectors of the disk. This gives the system the time it takes to pass over one sector to digest the previous block of data and get ready to read the next one. This is less demanding on the system, and is more easily achieved. However, it is still beyond the capabilities of many PC and hard disk combinations. A higher interleave factor is therefore needed in many cases, with (say) every seventh sector being used, representing an interleave factor of 7.

Determining the optimum interleave factor for a particular hard disk, controller, and PC combination is best done using a special test program. Unfortunately, these can be difficult to track down. At least one popular make of AT BIOS chip includes such a program in its built-in testing and diagnostic program, but apart from this I have not encountered such a program. Trying various interleave factors and then running performance tests is an alternative, but this is likely to prove a very time consuming business in practice. For a fast AT type computer with a special controller card a factor of 1 is obviously appropriate. Most ATs with ordinary hard disk controllers provide optimum results with an interleave factor of 3. The optimum for XTs and compatibles is more variable, but a value of 6 is usually about right.

Hard Cards

The easiest way of adding a hard disk to a PC is to use a "hard-card". This is a hard disk and controller on a standard full length PC expansion card. These are often described as something like "one and a half cards", which does not mean that they are 50% longer than a full length expansion card! It means that the front end of the card (where the hard disk is usually situated) is quite wide, preventing a card from being inserted into the adjacent expansion slot. In most cases a short card can be fitted into the next slot, and hence the hard cards are mostly "one and a half" size cards rather than "double" size types.

There are definite advantages in using a hard card, and

they have been quite popular over the last few years. Although at one time they were relatively expensive, these days they seem to be roughly comparable in price to an ordinary hard disk and controller of similar capacity and performance. Installation is very easy, being little more difficult than adding an ordinary expansion card. There is no need to worry about obtaining suitable fixings for the drive. Setting everything up ready for use is also quite straightforward in most cases. Some hard cards are supplied ready for immediate use, while others require only a very simple setting up procedure. Virtually all hard cards seem to have low levels of power consumption, making them suitable for use in any PC, including early types having relatively puny power supply units. When adding a conventional hard disk drive to an early PC it is often necessary to fit a more hefty power supply unit. Depending on the particular hard card used, it may block up more expansion slots than a hard disk controller plus separate hard disk.

Hard cards are not without their drawbacks, but these are relatively minor. With the disk drive tucked away inside the computer, there is no disk drive light to let you know when disk accesses are taking place. This may seem like a very trivial point, but it is something that you tend to miss when it is not there! Probably the biggest drawback is that these cards are generally only suitable for use in PCs, not ATs, as they have a PC XT style hard disk controller. Apparently there are such things as AT hard cards, but I have never come across one of these. It is something that would seem to be better suited to XTs, which have the hard disk BIOS as part of the controller rather than on the motherboard. If you have an 8088 or 8086 based floppy disk or twin floppy disk PC, then a hard card probably represents the easiest way of adding a hard disk drive to it.

Chapter 4

DISPLAY ADAPTORS

I suppose that one of the greatest strengths of the PC family is its wide range of display types. Whereas most other microcomputers have the display circuit included on the main board, with no easy way (and possibly no way at all) of using an improved display, on the PCs the display circuit is on a standard expansion card. With built-in display circuits there is an understandable tendency for the designer to compromise between the number of graphics colours and resolution on the one hand, and cost on the other. This has often led to a display that is capable of reasonable colour graphics, but one which is not outstanding in this respect. A display of this type may seem to be a good compromise, but it is unnecessarily expensive for those who only require text, and is probably not going to satisfy those who require high resolution colour graphics for CAD, illustration work, etc. Some very promising computers have ended up as little more than games machines as a result of this.

With the PCs, if all you want is a simple text display, or relatively low resolution graphics, then there are low cost display boards to suit your needs. If you need something a bit more exotic, then there are high resolution colour and monochrome graphics boards available, and many of these are also capable of displaying such things as 132 column text. At the top end of the graphics market there are various "power" graphics boards, which include on-board "intelligence" that enables them to produce very high resolution multi-colour graphics, but still operate at very fast speeds.

There is a slight drawback to this versatility in that applications programs, particularly those that use graphics, must be capable of handling several types of display adaptor if they are to give optimum results with a wide range of PC configurations. Most graphics based PC applications programs include some sort of setup or installation program that enables them to work with any of the standard PC graphics boards, plus (usually) some of the non-standard types. The more advanced graphics cards invariably seem to have some backwards compatibility. In other words, they can emulate some or all of the standard graphics boards, and should be usable with any applications program. The extra resolution and (or) colours they are capable of producing might not be usable with all applications programs though.

In fact the more advanced graphics cards are often only usable with a select few of the most popular pieces of graphics software. You must always check on compatibility between your applications programs and any display board you are considering buying, but this is especially important with any non-standard graphics card. Advanced graphics cards are usually supplied with drivers for the more popular applications program. It is worth checking what (if any) software drivers are supplied with any graphics board in which you are interested. Even if your programs do not support the graphics card, it could be that you are in luck, and that the card supports the program.

Standards
There are several standard display boards, and by standard I suppose I mean display cards that conform to standards laid down by IBM. There are a number of "specials" which do not conform to the IBM standards, but we will not consider these in any great detail. Most users find that one of the ordinary display boards satisfies their requirements. If you require a very high resolution display, especially a multi-colour type, you will probably need to pay out a great deal of money. In fact a display board of this type plus a matching monitor can easily cost substantially more than the rest of the hardware in the system. Exactly what is available in the way of high resolution display cards, and the programs that are compatible with them, seems to be constantly changing.

It is a matter of consulting the computer press and local dealers in order to find out just what is available at the time you wish to purchase a display system. Do not overlook the alternative of an enhanced VGA board. As we shall see shortly, these offer a very cost effective solution to high resolution multi-colour graphics.

The original PCs had a monochrome text only display, known as the MDA (monochrome display adaptor) card. This board was a popular choice for some time, as it was quite inexpensive, gave a high quality text display, and the adaptor card included the bonus of a parallel printer port. The obvious drawback of this card was that it could not produce true graphics, and as software gradually became more graphics oriented, this type of display became less popular. These days it has to be regarded as obsolete. Display boards of this type are now something of a rarity, and few computers seem to have an MDA card as a display option.

There were two types of display which ousted the MDA type. One of these was the IBM CGA (colour graphics adaptor), while the other was the Hercules type, produced by the company of the same name. If we consider the official IBM offering first, this has several operating modes, but only four of them are used to any extent. The least used of these is almost certainly the 40 x 25 character text only mode. A text mode with only 40 characters per line is not much use for general purpose word processing and the like, but it does have its uses. It is useful as a text mode for those with poor eyesight, and is also much used in scientific applications, where the ability to easily and quickly note down data from a screen is often a great asset. For most text applications though, it is the 80 by 25 character mode that is used. The quality of the display in this mode seems to vary somewhat from one manufacturer to another. Some cards seem to have well formed characters and quite smooth scrolling, while other have somewhat confusing characters and (or) suffer from "snow" or severe screen flicker when scrolling.

In both text modes the card operates in colour. It is normally stated that there are sixteen colours available, but I think that this is not strictly true. This display uses the RGBI (red — green — blue — intensity) method. This gives eight basic colours, from black with all three primary colours switched off, to white with them all switched on. The intensity signal can be used to switch the colours to half brightness, which, on the face of it, turns the basic eight colours into a maximum of sixteen. However, as half intensity black is still black, according to my calculations this gives a maximum of fifteen colours.

The other two popular modes are graphics types. One of these is a multi-colour mode, but it only offers four colours (including the background colour). The resolution is 320 by 200 pixels, which makes it considerably less than high resolution. This mode is quite useful if well used by the software, and I used a CAD program with this display mode very successfully for some time. For many users the main objections to this mode is the limited choice of colour pallets. The standard set of colours is a black background plus white, magenta, and cyan. For many purposes the alternative colour pallet of black plus green, yellow, and red is preferable, but not always supported by the software. However, a few CGA cards seem to default to this alternative colour pallet.

The other graphics mode is a monochrome one offering a slightly improved resolution of 640 by 200 pixels. The 640 pixel horizontal resolution is actually quite respectable, and not bettered by most of the more recent PC graphics standards. The 200 pixel vertical resolution is less satisfactory though, and is no better than that available in the colour mode. This display standard undoubtedly offers quite good performance, but even in its day it was something less than state of the art.

While CGA displays are still much used, they are rapidly being rendered obsolete by the falling cost of higher resolution alternatives. At one time a CGA display was much cheaper than the higher resolution colour types as it required a low cost monitor with the relatively low scanning rate of 15.75 kHz, and required little RAM. Recently the cost of high resolution, high scan rate, colour monitors has fallen dramatically, as has the cost of RAM chips. Taken as a percentage of the overall cost of the system, this has led to the difference in cost between a computer with CGA graphics and a one having a higher resolution colour display being quite small. Many computers are no longer offered with a CGA display as an option, and the small additional cost of a more modern display would seem to be money well spent.

The Hercules display offers a good quality 80 by 25 character text display, plus what at the time it was launched was a very high resolution graphics display of 720 by 348 pixels. This is actually quite good resolution by current standards, although it must be borne in mind that both the text and graphics displays are of the monochrome variety. The text display is of good quality, and as colour is of real importance in few text applications (and considered undesirable by many), the lack of colour in the text mode is not really a great drawback. Colour is of more significance in graphics applications, but is by no means always a necessity.

Although the Hercules display standard is not an official IBM one, it has achieved considerable success, and is very well supported by applications programs. Any program which could potentially exploit the Hercules graphics mode is almost certain to actually have this as an option in its setup or installation program. The reasons for its success are not difficult to see. It offers good text and high resolution graphics, and the card is fitted with a parallel printer port. It is a direct replacement for the MDA card, and works with the same monitors as the MDA card. It offers a very low cost route to high resolution graphics, and if colour is not of importance to you, a Hercules (or compatible) graphics card is still a worthwhile investment.

High Resolution Colour
The shortcomings of the CGA standard led to the develop-

ment of the EGA (enhanced graphics adaptor) card. This offers the same modes as the CGA type, plus some higher resolution types. An often overlooked fact is that it offers improved performance in the standard 80 by 25 character text mode. Whereas CGA 80 column characters are made up from 8 by 8 pixel blocks, an EGA board uses 8 by 14 pixel blocks. This gives very neat looking text with a gap between rows of letters (on the CGA text display a descender on a lower case letter is apt to occasionally join straight onto a full height letter immediately below it). To my eyes at least, an EGA text display looks much neater and is easier to read than even the best of CGA text displays. As an alternative to the 80 by 25 character display, an EGA screen can use an 8 by 8 pixel matrix for characters, giving lower quality but some 43 lines of text per screen.

Probably most users buy an EGA display for its improved graphics capability rather than for its superior text display. The graphics capabilities of this board depend on the amount of RAM fitted, but in practice the full 256k of RAM invariably seems to be fitted. With 64k of RAM it is possible to obtain 640 by 350 pixel resolution in monochrome. The full 256k of RAM permits the same resolution to be obtained, but with sixteen colours chosen from a palette of 64 colours. This is the graphics mode in which an EGA board would normally be used.

An EGA card can be used with a MDA monitor, but only by using it in the MDA text mode. Similarly, it can operate with a CGA monitor, but it then provides little more than the standard CGA modes. It does in fact provide an enhanced graphics mode in the form of a 640 by 200 pixel 16 colour mode. This is a great improvement on the basic CGA modes, but it is a mode that seems to be supported by relatively little software. The vast majority of EGA users buy an EGA compatible monitor, and take advantage of the well supported 16 colour 640 by 350 pixel mode.

The EGA standard has now been somewhat overshadowed by the more recent VGA display (which is described next), and it has received a certain amount of criticism. In my experience it gives excellent results when used with decent software, whether in a text or graphics mode. For some graphics applications the limited choice of screen colours is a definite limitation, and for these a VGA is undoubtedly a better option. For business graphics and CAD an EGA display is extremely good, and does not look a great deal different to a VGA display used in its highest resolution mode. However, EGA boards seem to be much slower than VGA cards, giving very much slower screen redrawing with some software. With the difference in cost between EGA and VGA graphics systems seeming to grow narrower by the day, and the difference having all but disappeared already, EGA displays are not such an attractive proposition as they were quite a short time ago.

VGA

Unless you are only interested in text based applications, or only require monochrome graphics, the obvious choice for a PC display these days is a VGA (versatile graphics array) type. Even if you do only require text or monochrome graphics, a VGA display might still be the best option. There are low cost VGA monochrome monitors available which offer (usually) sixty-four shades of grey. One of the cheaper VGA cards plus one of these monitors provides excellent text and graphics, good compatibility with any PC software, and makes it easy to upgrade to colour if this should become necessary at some later date. You simply replace the monochrome monitor with a colour VGA type.

VGA cards can provide all the earlier IBM screen modes (MDA, CGA, and EGA), plus a Hercules emulation in most cases. When dealing with VGA cards you will often come across references to "BIOS level" and "register level" (or "hardware level") compatibility. VGA graphics are supported by software routines contained in the BIOS ROMs on the board. The idea is that software should control the graphics via these software routines, rather

101

than by directly writing data to, and directly reading data from, the registers of the hardware. This is much the same idea as the computer only being controlled via the operating system routines and the routines in the main BIOS. In practice it suffers from the same problem, with many software writers seeking faster operating speeds by getting their programs to directly control the hardware instead of going via the BIOS routines.

In theory, a VGA card that is BIOS compatible with the IBM original should be able to run any program without difficulty. In practice, a VGA compatible card which is not both BIOS and register level compatible is likely to give problems with some software. Unfortunately, there is no way of determining which software will run faultlessly and which will give problems, other than giving the programs a prolonged trial with the board in question. Most modern VGA compatible boards now claim BIOS and register level compatibility. While some sets of VGA test programs may actually find a few deficiencies in most boards, in practice software incompatibility problems seem to be quite rare. Any that do turn up are often quite minor, and do not necessarily render the software unusable.

There is a substantial difference between VGA monitors and those used with the other display boards mentioned so far. The other graphics standards operate with digital signals, which means that each signal is either on (at about 5 volts) or off (at about 0 volts). It is this factor that limits the number of colours available. The basic RGB system controls the red, green, and blue guns of the c.r.t. (cathode ray tube) in the monitor, enabling each one to be either turned on or switched off. This permits eight colours to be obtained. As explained previously, the CGA display boards are for use with RGBI monitors. The fourth signal enables the intensity of the three electron guns in the c.r.t. to be at either full intensity, or a much reduced intensity. This doubles the number of colours available to either 15 or 16, depending on how you look at things.

The EGA monitors considerably extend the RGBI idea, and have two signals to control each of the three electron guns. This gives four intensities per primary colour, and a maximum of 64 colours available. Only 16 colours can be displayed at any one time, but this is a limitation placed on the system by the 256k of memory, and not by the monitor and the system of controlling it.

Monitors used with VGA boards are of the analogue variety. These have the usual RGB inputs to control the red, green, and blue guns of the c.r.t. in the monitor. The intensity of each electron beam is proportional to the voltage applied to the corresponding input, giving an infinite range of intensities for each primary colour. This in turn gives an infinite range of available colours from an analogue monitor. In theory it is possible for any colour to be produced, but in reality the state of monitor technology places some restrictions on the colour range. However, an impressive range of colours can be generated, as can some outstanding graphics images.

Although a VGA monitor can produce an almost unlimited range of colours, a VGA card can not. Each output signal is produced by a six bit digital to analogue converter. In other words, the computer generates the intensity value for each primary colour as a set of six digital signals. These are converted to a range of 64 voltages by the digital to analogue converter. With 64 intensities for each of the primary colours, this gives a basic palette of no less than 262144 colours (64 x 64 x 64 = 262144). It has to be stressed that not all of these colours can be displayed simultaneously. In fact the board's 256k of memory restricts the maximum number of displayed colours to 256, and in the highest resolution mode only 16 different colours can be displayed at once.

The two popular VGA modes are 320 by 200 pixels in up to 256 colours, and 640 by 480 pixels in 16 colours. This second mode gives more vertical resolution than an EGA display, and a greater selection of colours to choose from. It only permits the same number of colours on the screen simultaneously though, and is in many respects not a great improvement on the EGA standard. The lower resolution mode may not seem to be very good, with a resolution that exactly matches the CGA colour mode. However, with some 256 colours available simultaneously, and 262144 colours to choose from, it is a vast improvement on the CGA colour mode.

The lack of resolution is a definite drawback, but intelligent use of a large number of colours can to a large extent cover up the lack of resolution. Graphics in this mode can have what is often described as a "photographic" quality, offering far greater realism than higher resolution modes that offer far fewer colours. This mode is therefore very popular for use with paint and animation programs, while the higher resolution is the one that would normally be used for CAD, business graphics, etc. A VGA display offers a good quality 80 by 25 character text mode, that is comparable to the EGA type.

Enhanced VGA

With the obvious exception of the Hercules monochrome graphics standards, the widely supported PC graphics standards have all been originated by IBM themselves. This situation seems to be changing slightly, and a number of graphics board manufacturers have agreed on an extension of the VGA standard, known by such names "enhanced" and "super" VGA. This offers a resolution of 800 by 600 pixels with a maximum of 16 colours on screen at once. Most of the so-called third party VGA boards now seem to offer this resolution, plus some other enhanced VGA modes in most cases.

A common enhanced VGA mode is one that offers 600 by 400 pixel resolution with up to 256 colours displayed simultaneously. This is about the maximum pixels/colours that the standard 256k of VGA RAM can accommodate. Results in this mode can be extremely impressive indeed, giving the type of display you would associate with a good quality television screen rather than a computer monitor. It provides virtually the same number of pixels as the higher resolution mode, plus all the colours of the lower resolution mode.

Another common mode is one which gives the full 640 plus 480 pixel resolution, together with the full complement of 256 on-screen colours. However, this mode requires more than the normal 256k of RAM, and is only available on boards that can take (and are fitted with) 512k of RAM. You might be wondering where all this video RAM fits into the PC's memory map. With 640k of base RAM, and a total address space of 1M (1024k), there would seem to be nowhere for 512k of video RAM. The video RAM actually fits in the 128k of address space immediately above the 640k of base RAM. Where an EGA or VGA board is fitted with more than 128k of RAM, the RAM is split into pages, with the pages of RAM being switched in and out as required. This is basically the same method that is utilized with EMS expanded memory, albeit in a much simplified form.

With 512k of video RAM it is possible to go well beyond the 640 by 480 by 256 colour mode mentioned previously. Many enhanced VGA boards now do so, and the one fitted in the computer I am using to prepare this book has a mode which provides 800 by 600 pixel resolution plus up to 256 colours at once. Results in this mode can be truly spectacular, giving the sort of graphics that not so long ago were only possible using very expensive graphics work stations.

Many boards also offer a higher resolution mode with fewer colours. The resolution is normally 1024 by 768 pixels with up to 16 colours (fewer colours than this on some boards). This sort of resolution is suitable for demanding d.t.p. and CAD applications, but in order to avoid eye strain and fully utilize such high resolution a fairly sizeable monitor is needed. These tend to be pretty large (especially on the front-to-back measurement), very heavy, and extremely expensive. For most purposes a resolution of 640 by 480 or 800 by 600 and a 14 inch monitor (or thereabouts) is a more practical and perfectly satisfactory solution.

The drawback of the enhanced modes is that they seem

to be something less than fully standardised. Selecting the 800 by 600 16 colour mode for one enhanced VGA board when running a setup or installation program does not seem to guarantee results with a different enhanced VGA board that supports this mode. Looking on the bright side, enhanced VGA boards are normally supplied with some disks that contain useful utilities plus drivers for popular software (typically GEM, Windows, Ventura, AutoCAD, Word Perfect, and Lotus 123). Also, many graphics programs now support the more popular of these cards, and support for them seems to be increasing. Their popularity is such that this trend seems likely to continue, or even to accelerate. Provided you obtain one of the more common enhanced VGA cards, or perhaps one that is based on the same chip set as a popular type, you are likely to find that it is well supported. As always though, it is advisable to get the software that suits your requirements, and to then purchase the hardware needed to make it function in the desired manner.

Monitors

Installing graphics cards is not usually too difficult. In most cases there will be a few jumper leads or DIP switches that must be set up in order to get the board to function in the correct start-up mode, or whatever. Many EGA and VGA boards have the ability to sense the graphics mode that the software is trying to use, and to then automatically switch to that display mode. This "intelligence" may be built into the board, or it may require a utility program to be run at start-up. Most boards also come complete with a utility program that enables the board to be forced into any desired text or graphics mode. There can sometimes be problems in getting a display card properly into the right mode. In some cases moving from one program to another is only possible if the computer is reset. This is not a problem that is confined to video cards though, and problems with mouse drivers and other "left-over" software utilities can force resetting of the computer when changing from one program to another.

Having chosen a graphics card, you need to be careful that the monitor you obtain will match it properly, and support the display modes that you will require. The most simple and inexpensive of the monitors for use with PCs are the Hercules/MDA compatible types. These are available in a variety of sizes and display colours (amber, green, and paper white), and are widely available.

The colour monitors for CGA displays are also widely available, but seem to be somewhat less common than they were a couple of years ago. Not all RGBI monitors are suitable for operation with CGA cards, since a few have a combined horizontal and vertical synchronisation input, whereas the CGA card provides separate synchronisation signals. The PC compatible RGBI variety is by far the more common though, and provided you buy a monitor described as PC compatible, it should just be a matter of connecting its 9 pin D type plug into the socket on the CGA card. There are monochrome monitors that are compatible with CGA cards, but a CGA card plus monochrome monitor is often a rather less than entirely satisfactory combination. Display clarity is often not all that one would desire, and although the different colours should be displayed as different intensities, in practice there is often little difference between them.

An EGA board requires a special monitor which, as far as I am aware, is only used with the PC and this type of display adaptor. These are mostly of the colour variety, but there are some monochrome monitors that are compatible with the EGA standard. Some of these are dual standard monitors, that can operate with either MDA/Hercules boards, or EGA cards. I can not claim to have seen an EGA monochrome monitor in action, but by most reports they provide quite acceptable results.

For VGA card users there are likely to be a number of options available. Some VGA cards are fitted with both the 9 pin D connector (as used on earlier PC display cards) and the 15 pin D connector that is the standard for VGA boards. This means that they can operate with any PC compatible monitor that has the correct 9 pin connector.

However, only the modes supported by the monitor will be available, and this means that the colours and high resolution of the VGA card will be unobtainable. Consequently, there would seem to be little point in using a monitor of this type with a VGA board, and the inclusion of a 9 pin connector on VGA cards seems to be a feature that is dying out.

The lowest cost option that gives access to the advanced modes of a VGA card is a monochrome VGA monitor. As mentioned previously, this gives 64 grey levels instead of up to 256 colours. It does not represent an ideal solution for someone who will be running paint programs etc. in the 320 by 200 pixel 256 colour mode. It does represent a very cost effective solution if your main interest is running d.t.p. software in the 640 by 480 pixel 16 colour mode. Grey levels rather than different colours is often all that is required in an application of this type.

There is a similar option in the form of "multisync" monochrome monitors. As their name suggests, multisync monitors can adjust themselves, or be manually set, to operate with a range of graphics standards. In most cases they can operate with logic or analogue input signals, and are supplied with an adaptor that permits them to be connected to either a 9 pin or a 15 pin D type connector. Some multisync monochrome monitors can not scan at the higher rates needed to accommodate modes beyond a resolution of 640 by 480 pixels.

Although these may not seem to offer any advantage over a straightforward VGA monochrome monitor, they may in fact do so. A normal VGA monitor can not operate properly with CGA signals etc. CGA and other non-VGA modes are produced using an emulation process which produces what looks very much like "the real thing", but is actually quite different. In the CGA 320 by 200 pixel mode for instance, each line is actually produced by two scans across the screen. The display is actually a 320 by 400 pixel type, but with the lines in identical pairs it looks much like a true 320 by 200 pixel type.

For most purposes the emulated display modes, which are not likely to be needed much anyway, should be perfectly satisfactory. Some VGA cards can produce the proper modes though, but a multisync monitor is needed in order to display them. Note that most VGA boards do not seem to include any form of Hercules emulation, but can usually produce a proper Hercules compatible output. If you require a monochrome VGA system that can provide Hercules compatible graphics, then you will almost certainly need a monochrome multisync monitor in order to achieve this.

The cheapest form of colour monitor for a VGA display is the type which is normally described simply as an "analogue" or "VGA" monitor. These are both rather vague terms, but in a PC context they mean a monitor which has analogue RGB inputs via the standard 15 pin D type connector, and which can scan at the standard VGA frequencies. This type of monitor is adequate for most purposes, giving access to the 320 by 200 pixel 256 colour mode, and the 640 by 480 pixel 16 colour mode. It does have its limitations though, in that it will probably not be possible to display Hercules style graphics, and any enhanced VGA modes supported by the VGA card which go beyond the 640 by 480 pixel resolution will be outside the scanning range of the monitor. Trying to display modes at resolutions beyond the official scanning range of a monitor is definitely not a good idea. It could result in damage to the monitor due to certain components overheating (although most modern monitors now seem to include cut-out circuits to guard against this problem).

A relatively recent development in monitors is a dual standard VGA analogue type. These are effectively standard VGA monitors which have the ability to switch (usually automatically) to a higher scan rate so that they can display the enhanced VGA modes which provide 800 by 600 pixel resolution. It should perhaps be pointed out that you do not need a special VGA monitor to display the enhanced modes that provide 640 by 400 pixels or

109

640 by 480 pixels in 256 colours. Any analogue colour monitor should be capable of displaying the full colour range of the graphics card, no matter how many colours that happens to be. One of these dual standard VGA monitors is therefore quite capable of displaying the 800 by 600 pixel 256 colour mode if it is supported by the VGA card.

At the top end of the VGA monitor market are the true multisync colour monitors. A monitor of this type will usually be compatible with any PC graphics card from the MDA type through to a VGA card operating in an 800 by 600 pixel mode. Unless you actually need full compatibility with pre VGA modes a multisync monitor of this type offers no advantage over a dual standard VGA type. Some multisync monitors can now operate right up to the 1024 by 768 pixel enhanced VGA resolution.

There is a potential problem here in that some graphics systems which operate at this resolution use interlacing, but others do not. Interlacing is where every other line is scanned on the first frame, then the missing lines are scanned on the next frame. Two frames (i.e. two scans of the screen) are therefore needed per complete screenful. This method uses a lower scanning rate which puts less stringent requirements on the components in the monitor. The lower scan rate tends to give a certain amount of screen flicker though, and the interlacing helps to mini- mise this. Anyway, if you are contemplating a graphics system which makes use of a 1024 by 768 pixel mode, you need to make careful enquiries in order to make quite sure that the graphics card and monitor you select are properly compatible.

When looking at monitor specifications you will often encounter the term "dot pitch". In theory, the smaller the dot pitch, the higher the display quality is likely to be. In reality matters are not as straightforward as this, and two monitors having the same claimed dot pitch might actually give significantly different display qualities. The claimed size of the screen is something that is sometimes a bit over-optimistic. There are 14 inch monitors available that have a significant area around the border of the screen that is unused (and unusable). These are often described as something like "14 inch screen (13 inch visible)". They really have to be regarded as 13 inch (or whatever) monitors, rather than 14 inch types.

Even with true 14 inch screens you often find that a fair sized border is left unused around the edges of the screen. Most monitors allow the vertical size of the display to be adjusted so that it can be made to fill out the screen in this direction, but an equivalent control for the horizontal direction is something of a rarity. Where such a control is fitted, it is often in the form of a switch that provides normal and wide settings. This is a very useful feature indeed, and can help to make the most of the available screen area. The difference in the size of the actual displays on two supposedly 14 inch monitors can be quite surprising. For some reason, the display often seems to noticeably shrink when a dual standard VGA or multisync monitor switches to the 800 by 600 pixel mode. This can result in a very disappointing display area with some monitors.

There is a great deal to be said for actually seeing your chosen display card and monitor in action before you go ahead and buy them. If there should just happen to be any form of incompatibility problem, then a practical test of the two together should bring it to light. Perhaps of equal or greater importance, it will enable you to assess the display quality to ascertain whether or not it meets your requirements. If the display area is a lot smaller than you expected, there will be an opportunity to change your mind before parting with any money. On the other hand, if the display quality is "crisp" and the colours are good, you might be quite happy with a comparatively small display area. This type of thing is very much a matter of personal preference, and something that you must decide for yourself.

For reference purposes, a list of the standard IBM graphics modes (plus the Hercules modes) are provided overleaf. The frequency quoted is the horizontal scan

Mode	Text Res.	Graphics Res.	Colours	Display Card	Frequency
0	40 x 25		2	MDA	18.43
1	40 x 25		16	CGA	15.75
2	80 x 25		2	MDA	18.43
3	80 x 25		16	CGA	15.75
4		320 x 200	4	CGA	15.75
5		320 x 200	2	CGA	15.75
6		640 x 200	2	CGA	15.75
13		320 x 200	16	EGA	15.75
14		640 x 200	16	EGA	15.75
15		640 x 350	2	EGA	22.00
16		640 x 350	16	EGA	22.00
17		640 x 480	2	VGA	31.50
18		640 x 480	16	VGA	31.50
19		320 x 200	256	VGA	31.50
	80 x 25		2	Hercules	18.43
		720 x 348	2	Hercules	18.43

frequency in kilohertz, and could be useful when checking monitor compatibility with a given display card. The vertical scan rates are 50 Hz for MDA/Hercules modes, 60 Hz for CGA and EGA modes, and 70 Hz for VGA modes.

Mention should perhaps be made of the IBM PGA (professional graphics adaptor) board. This is actually a board set and matching monitor which provides 640 x 480 graphics resolution. Although this may seem to be no better than a VGA board, there is a difference in that the PGA board has a built-in microprocessor and some specialised hardware that enable it to take over much of the complex calculating associated with the manipulation of high resolution graphics images. This permits very fast operation for 3D CAD programs and the like, but the PGA system was quite expensive. Consequently it never achieved widespread use, and was only targeted at specialist applications.

It is perhaps worth mentioning that PCs can operate with two displays running simultaneously. However, this is normally only possible if one display is a monochrome text type and the other is a colour graphics type. This might seem to be an interesting but useless feature, but it does have its uses. A number of CAD programs can operate in this dual screen mode, with menus displayed on the text screen and the drawing displayed on the graphics screen. This leaves all the graphics screen for the drawing, but with a full text screen for the menus, it also permits a large number of menus to be displayed at once. This gives instant access to a large number of options without the need for large numbers of pop-down menus, sub-menus, and sub-sub-menus. I can not claim to have used this system, but it is one which seems to be favoured by a significant number of people who are professional users of CAD software or other complex graphics programs.

Chapter 5

PC REPAIRS

There is an old joke about the woman who was amazed that her old broom had lasted thirty years — and it only needed two new handles and seven new heads! I suppose that the modular construction of PCs leaves them open to the same sort of claim. Over the years you can put in a new display card here, a replacement disk drive there, and maybe even a new motherboard in the fullness of time. Five or six years later the computer will still be going strong, and will probably have a specification well above that of the original machine, but the case might be the only survivor from the original hardware!

The PC's modular method of construction aids the DIY repairer. Even if you can not mend the particular item that is faulty, then it can instead be completely replaced. This might seem to be a wasteful approach, and to an extent I suppose that it is. Being realistic about modern electronics in general, current production processes are so efficient that many pieces of equipment can now be produced at very low cost. Repairing equipment can take a lot of man hours from highly skilled (and well paid) service engineers, making it a costly process. Modern production processes are designed to make the manufacture of equipment as cheap as possible, with servicing usually being of only secondary importance. This makes fitting replacement parts on some circuit boards quite difficult.

Obviously each case has to be assessed on its own merits. Throwing away a high capacity hard disk drive that has become faulty just outside the guarantee period and replacing it with a new one would not be a cost effective way of handling the problem. At the other extreme, something like a parallel printer port card that has become faulty after several years use is probably not worth repairing. It would only cost a few pounds to replace it with a new one.

There is a big incentive to undertake DIY repairs. The cost of professional repairs on PCs can be quite high, with the minimum fee sometimes being higher than the cost of any one of an average PCs component parts. Carriage costs to and from the service centre can be high, as can calling in an engineer to provide on-site maintenance. While I would not advocate prodding around inside expensive computer equipment if you are not reasonably practical, and have little knowledge about PCs, a lot of PC maintenance is within the capabilities of anyone who is reasonably practical, and does know about the general make up and operation of these computers.

In this chapter we will consider some common problems with PCs (which also apply to computers in general in most cases), plus ways of detecting and correcting these faults. As already intimated, we will mainly be concerned with locating the faulty device so that it can be replaced, rather than locating and repairing the faulty module. Where appropriate, repairs on faulty sections of the computer will be described though, and the subject of preventive maintenance will also be discussed. The old saying "prevention is better than cure" is just as applicable to PCs as it is to anything else.

Hard Disks

In my experience of PCs, all of which have been equipped with hard disk drives, these are the most likely cause of problems. This is perhaps not surprising when you consider their electronic and mechanical complexity. It is a tribute to the hard disk manufacturers that these units are as reliable as they are. Most units give at least a couple of years service before any problems emerge.

There seems to be a popular misconception that problems with hard disk drives are almost invariably due to weaknesses in the magnetic coatings of the disks themselves, and that reformatting etc. will usually effect a cure. It is true that problems can often be solved by what is basically a reformatting of the disk, and this is a subject we will pursue shortly. However, it must be pointed out that there are a fair percentage of cases where this will provide no improvement whatever. Being complex mechanical devices, hard disks are naturally prone to mechanical failures. If you take a faulty disk drive and slowly roll it over in your hands, any noise caused by bits of metal (or whatever) rattling around inside the unit almost certainly indicates that there is a serious mechanical problem with the drive.

Even if there is no evidence of anything loose inside the drive, it might still have mechanical problems. In this case, and unless there are any other signs of mechanical problems, the obvious option is to first try reformatting the drive. If this fails to effect an improvement, then the fault is almost certainly a mechanical problem with the drive. Of course, there are some complex control electronics built into every hard disk drive, and the problem could lay here. This is unlikely, as modern electronics have a very high degree of reliability. In a way it is purely academic as to whether the problem is mechanical or in the control electronics. Either way a DIY repair is almost certainly out of the question. You should definitely not open up a hard disk drive to look inside. These devices are sealed to keep out dust, as dust particles can easily cause serious damage to the surface of the disk if they should come between the heads and the rapidly rotating disks.

If reformatting will not effect a cure, there is little option to returning the disk drive to the dealer or manufacturer for repairs. If the disk drive is a few years old and not a very expensive type, it might be better to simply fit a new unit. Getting the old one repaired could cost nearly as much, and will leave you with a disk drive that has had a substantial amount of wear. A new unit might cost a little more, but should give several years of trouble-free operation. While it might seem that having the old unit repaired will bring the advantage of leaving the contents of the disk intact, this is not actually the case. You might be lucky and have the disk returned with all the data and programs intact. This is unlikely though, since hard disk repairs often involve test and setting up procedures that leave the original contents of the disk largely or wholly erased. Any important data on a hard disk should always be backed-up on floppy disks or tape. Any remotely serious problem with a hard disk is almost certain to result in a total loss of the information stored on the disk.

I will not go into detail here about reformatting hard disk drives, since this is essentially the same as formatting a newly installed hard disk, which has already been described. You effectively pretend that the disk is a blank type and that you are starting from scratch with it. Both low and high level formats are therefore performed. Although reformatting may not seem to bring any advantages, it can in fact do so.

Drives that are based on stepper motors (which includes a number of very popular types) can have problems with the drive gradually slipping out of alignment. Rather than adjusting the drive to bring it back into alignment, it can be reformatted so that the tracks etc. are moved to new positions that suit the mechanics of the drive. Another problem that can occur is that of the magnetic signal on the disk gradually becoming weaker. Reformatting the disk will result in all the information, including track and sector marker signals, being refreshed, and returned to their original strength.

It is tempting to think of magnetic recordings of any type as being permanent. This is definitely not the case though. Although magnetic recordings seem to be long lived, they are finite, and any important information on floppy or hard disk should be refreshed at least every few years. An advantage of a digital recording, such as computer data stored on disk, is that it can be copied over and over again with no loss of quality. Provided fresh copies are made in time, data can be stored in this form indefinitely. Some people recommend periodic reformatting of hard disks and restoring of the backed-up programs and data. This is certainly a good idea, but the time involved is such that I doubt if many PC users actually bother to do this.

If the problem with the hard disk is due to the disks having developed some weak spots in their magnetic coatings, reformatting might not be much use. To sort out this type of thing some hard disk diagnostics software is required, and there is plenty of this in existence. Some computers are supplied together with some useful diagnostics utilities, and some BIOSs have some very useful built-in diagnostic routines. If suitable software was not included with your PC, a check through some shareware/ PD software ctalogues will probably reveal some programs that "fit the bill". Shareware software is ideal for this type of thing since it costs you little to try it out, and you are under no legal or moral obligation to register your copy if it turns out to be of no help. Some of these programs are quite advanced, and will effectively check the disk and take any necessary action if weak spots are found. Others simply tell you if an error of some kind is found, with at least a brief run down on the nature of the fault being provided.

You can not totally rule out the possibility of the disk controller being faulty. Some hard disk test programs will run a check on the controller and report any errors that are found. One of the best methods of checking for faults in modular equipment is to use substitution. In this context, you could try swopping the hard disk controllers of two computers of comparable types. If the fault moves across from one computer to another, then the problem is clearly due to the controller being faulty. You could obviously try the same method with the hard disk itself, although this would be a bit time consuming. If swapping the hard disk controllers does not result in the fault migrating from one computer to the other, it is virtually certain that the problem is in the hard disk itself.

It would not completely ensure that the problem was in the hard disk, as there is also the connecting cables to consider. Problems with cables, and not just hard disk cables, are not exactly a rarity. Problems are most likely to occur with cables such as printer types, which are external to the computer where they can easily get kicked, trodden on, or otherwise disturbed. Internal cables are not immune to problems though, and these can easily arise if you need to start delving around in the computer in order to add a new card, if you move the computer to a new location, or something of this nature. They can occasionally happen for no apparent reason whatever. This is presumably where one wire in a cable is damaged and barely making a connection. In the fullness of time it may corrode slightly, eventually resulting in its complete failure. The vibration from the cooling fan in the power supply unit and vibration from the disk drives could presumably result in things wearing loose over a period of time, with the connection between a plug and cable eventually failing as a result.

In order to check cables some form of continuity tester is required. This can be something as basic as the old torch bulb and battery setup at one extreme, or an expensive digital multimeter set to a low resistance range at the other extreme. In either case the cables should be completely removed from the hard disk and controller (or whatever) before checking for continuity between the connectors. Modern electronic components are often delicate devices which can be damaged by quite low voltages and currents. Fully disconnecting the cable prior to testing it ensures that there is no risk of the continuity tester damaging any of the computer's delicate electronics. If the cable is a floppy or hard disk type which has the "twist", remember that some of the connections between the connectors at the ends of the cable will be reversed.

If a cable is found to be faulty, and it is an IDC type, it will probably be possible to effect a cure by carefully removing the connectors, cutting about 20 millimetres from each end of the cable, and then refitting the connectors. Take due care when removing the connectors, as the metal terminals can tend to adhere to the wires and part company with the body of the connector, whereas it is the opposite of this that is required. This removal and replacement of the connectors might seem to be a waste of time, but it is often very effective. The most likely place for one of the wires to be damaged is where it enters the connector. Removing a connector, shortening the cable slightly, and then replacing the connector is likely to cut out the faulty piece of cable, and cure the problem. Often the cause of the fault is a poor connection between the cable and the connector. Removing the connector and refitting it will give a fresh set of connections, and may well clear the trouble.

I have experienced problems with disk drive cables that have connectors for two drives, where the connector for the second drive (i.e. the one that is some way in from the end of the cable) cuts through one or more of the wires. This prevents some of the signals from reaching the first drive. Continuity checks will show up this type of thing, since the connector for the second drive will not be in full electrical contact with one of the other connectors. With this type of fault it is best to obtain a new length of cable, rather than trying to repair the old one (which is never likely to be completely reliable).

Floppy Disks

Although largely mechanical in nature, modern floppy disk drives, in my experience at least, are very reliable. The same is not necessarily true of the floppy disks themselves. In fact any good quality disks from a reputable manufacturer should, unless you are very unlucky, give trouble-free operation for a considerable period of time. Many of the cheaper disks are also of very good quality, but there are some which seem to fall short of a satisfactory level of performance. If you experience disk errors when reading from and writing to inexpensive floppy disks, but the drive shows no obvious signs of any mechanical troubles, it is likely that it is the disks that are faulty and not the drive. The "acid test" is to try the drive with some good quality disks to see if any reading or writing problems are experienced with media that is known not to be sub-standard.

Floppy disk drives are a good example of something where some simple preventive maintenance is well worthwhile. With floppy disk drives the recording/playback head comes into contact with the disk, as it does with ordinary audio tape and cassette recorders. In common with audio magnetic recording, this results in a certain amount of the oxide coating being rubbed off the media and onto the heads. This can build up over a period of time, resulting in both a gradual decrease in the level of the signal recorded onto the disk, and a weaker signal being read from the disk. Inevitably, this eventually results in difficulties in reading data from disks.

The use of a floppy disk drive cleaner will often result in the disks being perfectly readable again. The heads of a disk drive are often difficult to get at, especially the surfaces from which the oxide must be cleaned away. A floppy disk drive cleaner offers a quick and easy way of cleaning the heads. The type I have used successfully for some time looks very much like an ordinary floppy disk, but the disk part is actually made from an absorbent substance onto which some of the cleaning fluid (supplied as part of the cleaning kit) is placed. It is then placed in the disk drive in the usual way, and you get the computer to do several seconds worth of disk accesses (by trying to get it to list a directory for the head cleaner for instance!).

This is such a fast and simple method of cleaning the heads that it does not really make sense to wait until problems are experienced before using the cleaning kit. Cleaning the heads (say) every month or two should ensure that dirty heads do not cause any read/write problems. It should also ensure that a good strong signal is always placed onto your floppy disks, ensuring that they will remain readable for a long period of time. Some head cleaner manufacturers seem to recommend very frequent use of their products. In my experience, unless you make very intensive use of the floppy disk drives, using a cleaner only every month or two should be quite sufficient.

Remember that 360k disks produced on a 1.2 megabyte

drive are often not readable on a 360k drive. Many PC users have thought that their disk drive is faulty when the problem is simply that they are trying to get it to read a disk that is totally unreadable on that particular type of drive. Also remember that while a 360k drive might not be able to read a disk of this type, this does not mean that the disk is totally unreadable. 360k disks produced on 1.2 megabyte drives are usually perfectly readable on any 1.2 megabyte disk drive.

In a similar vein, make sure that you use the right type of floppy disk for each drive. As you would expect, the ordinary 360k disks (40 track, double sided, double density types) are not of a high enough standard to be used as 1.2 megabyte types. Perhaps less well appreciated is the fact that high density 1.2 megabyte disks are not suitable for use with 360k drives. Although they have magnetic coatings of a very high standard, they are designed to take the lower power signals used by 1.2 megabyte drives. They can not properly handle the stronger signals produced by 360k drives, and tend to give an inadequate signal level when read-back by one of these drives. Always use the right type of floppy disk, not whatever happens to come to hand, or what you can get cheap at the time.

Take good care of floppy disks as they are easily damaged. Definitely do not bend floppy disks. This can result in the coating parting company with the base material, as can high or low storage temperatures (due to the base material and coating not expanding and contracting by the same amount). Writing on the label using a ballpoint pen or a hard pencil is another good way of damaging the coating!

Touching the surface of the disk can damage the coating, or result in dirt sticking to it and possibly causing damage the next time the disk is used. Dirt on the disk will not do the heads a great deal of good either. Spilling things onto a disk is a popular way of damaging them, but you might actually find that the disk is readable once it has dried out. However, if a disk is badly contaminated, it would be advisable not to fit it into the drive at all. The contamination could easily be picked up by the heads, possibly damaging them, and any disks subsequently used in the drive.

Of course, magnetic fields can alter the data on the disks, and must be avoided. In the short term, only strong magnetic fields would be likely to have any effect, but note that in the long term relatively weak fields could possibly have a detrimental affect on the disks. Powerful magnets are to be found in most loudspeakers, plus virtually anything that uses a small d.c. electric motor. Many electrical appliances contain some form of electro-magnet that produces varying magnetic fields when the device is in use, and these are probably more hazardous to floppy disks than the fixed fields produced by permanent magnets.

If the floppy disk drive is definitely faulty, and the problem is not the disks themselves, fitting a replacement should not prove to be too difficult. You could opt for trying to have the faulty unit repaired, but this is likely to prove quite costly. Even having a unit that has gone out of alignment realigned is not likely to be cost effective. Provided the replacement drive is one specifically intended for PC use, it will almost certainly be supplied with the configuration switches etc. already setup correctly. Disk drive chassis have standardised mounting holes, and the original screws, mounting rails, etc. should be perfectly suitable for the new drive. If the drive being replaced is drive B, remember that its set of terminating resistors should be removed or switched out of circuit, as appropriate.

Memory

A standard feature of all PC BIOSs is a set of test routines at switch-on or when the computer is reset. Some of these test routines seem to be very thorough, often taking an inordinate amount of time. Others are quite brief, but they all include a memory test (but note that this test is not run after a software reset of the Ctrl-Alt-Del type). Memory chips are highly complex devices that are generally accepted as being more prone to failure than most of the other components on the motherboard. The power-on self-test program will tell you if there is a problem, but it is unlikely to give you much help in locating the particular chip that is faulty. There are diagnostic programs available which might give more help, and you should not overlook the numerous useful diagnostic programs that are in the public domain, and are readily available at very low cost from most PC public domain/shareware suppliers. The DIY PC repairer should arm him or herself with as much diagnostic software as possible.

Gadgets for testing memory chips are available, but are very expensive and are not a practical proposition for the DIY PC repairer. The best RAM chip tester in this context is probably the PC itself. Finding the offending chip often comes down to swopping the suspect chip for a new one. If that does not eliminate the problem, try again with another chip, and so on, until the fault is found. Replacing chips one at a time is going to be a very time consuming process unless you find the faulty device early on in the proceedings. This will not always be the case, since the diagnostic software may not permit you to narrow down the offending component to one particular chip. Chips should only be removed or inserted into their socket when the computer is switched off.

It is more practical to have at least four or five spare memory chips so that you can find the offending memory chip reasonably quickly even if you have to methodically replace every memory chip on the motherboard! A problem with this method is that you will be left with four or five chips, one of which will be faulty, but you will have no way of knowing which one. You could simply discard the lot, or you can try each one in turn on the motherboard to find out which one is faulty. Whether or not this is worthwhile depends on whether the chips concerned are very cheap components or one of the more expensive types.

If a memory error is reported, it does not definitely mean that one of the memory chips is faulty. The problem could be due to a mechanical fault on the circuit board, but this is extremely unlikely. A much more common cause of memory problems is a chip that is not making good contact with its socket. PC memory chips are normally mounted in sockets so that it is easy to replace a chip, or to change the memory configuration if more than one type of chip is supported. Incidentally, it is very difficult to replace a memory chip if it is soldered to the board, and this is something that only an experienced service engineer should attempt. If a memory problem should occur, it is often worthwhile simply removing all the chips from their sockets, and carefully replacing them. Ideally some contact cleaner should be used to clean the sockets before the memory chips are replaced. However, any bad contacts will almost certainly be cured simply by removing and replacing the memory chips. The main advantage of the contact cleaner is in delaying any reoccurrence of the problem.

If you try this you obviously need to be reasonably careful. Memory integrated circuits are static sensitive devices, and should only be handled where there is no obvious danger from high static voltages. Make a note of their orientation before removing them, preferably making a sketch to help ensure that no careless mistakes are made when they are replaced. Integrated circuits should be removed by gently levering them free using a miniature screwdriver, taking care not to bend any of the pins. They must be carefully reinserted into their sockets, making quite sure that they are fitting the right way round, that none of the pins are buckled underneath them, and that none of the pins slip outside the socket instead of into the metal contacts.

With many new PCs now making use of SIMMs, correcting a memory fault becomes much easier. You simply replace the faulty SIMM, and the diagnostic program may even make it clear which SIMM should be replaced. The price you pay for this convenience is that one faulty chip will result in a whole bank of nine being replaced. With SIMMs using miniature surface mount chips that are soldered in place using special production techniques, there is little realistic prospect of repairing a standard SIMM.

Keyboard

I suppose that heavy users of PCs should regard keyboards as analogous to the tyres of a car — they will gradually wear out and need periodic replacement. If a keyboard has been given several years of hard use it is probably not worth repairing it, even if it is repairable. You can tend to find that no sooner have you repaired one fault than another one turns up. Although a PC keyboard contains some sophisticated electronics (it actually contains its own single-chip microcomputer), keyboard problems are almost invariably due to mechanical faults. If one part of the keyboard has sustained sufficient wear to render it inoperative, there are probably numerous other keys etc. on the brink of developing faults.

Replacing a keyboard has to be the most simple of PC repairs. You simply unplug the old one and plug-in the replacement. If the new keyboard is not an auto-sensing type, there will be a switch that must be set to the "XT" or "AT" position, depending on the type of computer in question. You may feel inclined to upgrade from an old 84 key type to the new enhanced 102 key type if the faulty unit has the old layout. Bear in mind that an old BIOS is very unlikely to respond properly to all the extra keys properly. Probably the keys of most interest are the separate cursor keys, plus "Insert", "Home", etc. These will almost certainly work perfectly. The "F11" and "F12" function keys will probably not work at all or give the wrong functions, and some of the other keys may need the aid of a keyboard redefinition program in order to get them to function properly. There can also be problems with one of the "lock" key indicator lights not initially responding properly. The safest course of action is to replace the old keyboard with a new one that is of exactly the same type.

Keyboards can certainly benefit from preventive maintenance and lack of abuse. A drink accidentally spilled onto a keyboard will probably ruin it, and this is not exactly an unknown occurrence. This does not necessarily leave the keyboard beyond repair, and if the actual

127

keyboard section of the unit is removed, cleaning it in large amounts of water (preferably of the distilled variety) and thoroughly drying it may well remove all the contamination and leave it fully functioning. This is likely to be a quite time consuming business though. I would recommend that no attempt should be made to dismantle the actual keyboard part of the unit. Methods of construction vary considerably from one manufacturer to another, but with many PC keyboards it is easy to end up with heaps of small springs and bits of metal, with no easy way of putting everything back together again.

The standard maintenance for a computer keyboard is to simply vacuum it every few months. This is very effective since it keeps dust and fluff away from the contacts. If any dust should get into the keyswitches, it can easily prevent the moving contact from touching and bridging the two fixed contacts. The switches are usually of sealed construction so that there is no easy way of dust entering, but given enough dust and a long enough period of time it is possible that problems could result. Probably a bigger danger is that so much dust and fluff will accumulate around the switch caps that their travel will be restricted to the point where some of the keys fail to make reliable contact. It is much easier to never let things build up to this point rather than to have to dig out all the fluff and dirt once things have gone too far.

If a keyboard has one or two keys that are unreliable, or one of the keys is effectively stuck in the down position, then it is virtually certain that the problem lies in the keyswitches. If it simply fails to work at all, produces random characters, or something of this nature, then the problem almost certainly lies in the electronics or the connecting cable. The latter is the most likely cause of problems. Fitting a new cable is unlikely to be too difficult. Removing about half a dozen screws from the base of the unit is normally all that is needed in order to give access to the interior of the keyboard. In some cases the cable attaches to the printed circuit board via a connector, but sometimes it is necessary to desolder the five leads and then solder in the replacement.

Display and Ports

If there is a fault in the display card or monitor, this should be immediately apparent. Things are not always what they seem though, and a fault in some other part of the computer could cause a crash which would leave a blank screen, or perhaps a screen full of "garbage". Also, even if it is the display section of the computer that is at fault, it will probably not be apparent whether the problem lies in the display card or the monitor (unless there is smoke coming from the latter of course!). There are plenty of display test programs, but these are obviously only usable if the display is to some extent operational. This type of software will probably not enable you to sort out whether it is the display card or the monitor at fault.

This is another example of the substitution method of fault finding offering the best chance of finding the faulty section of the computer. If you can swop the monitors of the faulty PC and another PC, and provided the monitors are of comparable types, this will show whether it is the display card or the monitor which is faulty. If the faulty PC produces a proper display, then it is the monitor that is faulty. If the problem is transferred to the other computer, then it is the display card that is faulty.

Most monitors and some display cards are quite expensive items. Faulty units of this type, unless they are several years old, may well be worth having repaired. Due to the rather specialised nature of display cards, the chances of repairing one successfully yourself are minimal (especially as so many of them now make extensive use of minute surface mount components). Monitors operate with extremely high voltages in parts of their circuits, and these high voltages are often retained for a long time after the unit has been switched off. This makes servicing them extremely dangerous, and something that should only be undertaken by a properly qualified service engineer. Both display cards and monitors often seem to have longer than normal guarantee periods. It is therefore worth checking the date of purchase and guarantee period even if the faulty display card or monitor is a few years old.

Do not overlook the possibility that the problem is due to a faulty monitor cable. If moving the cable around and pulling on it gently results in the correct display appearing intermittently, this almost certainly indicates a faulty cable or connector. Incorrect screen colours can also be caused by a faulty cable, with the signal for one of the primary colours not getting through to the monitor. However, this fault can also result from a faulty display card or monitor.

There are numerous pieces of software available for testing the serial and parallel ports of a PC. These operate in a variety of ways, such as sending test pieces of text to a printer, checking the registers of the ports, and getting a serial port to transmit data to itself using various baud rates and word formats. Routines of this type can be helpful, but they may not pin-point the exact fault. Once again, the best method of tracking down the faulty piece of gear is to use the substitution method. Remember that a serial or parallel port card set up for one computer might need to be reconfigured in order to use it in another computer. Do not forget to try swopping the leads as well as the cards. The connecting lead is probably the most likely cause of the problem. Also, do not overlook the fact that the fault might lie in the equipment at the end of the cable, not the PC itself.

Power Supply
The power supply has to be rated as an item which is relatively likely to fail. If a PC fails to operate at all, suspect the mains lead, plug and fuse first, and only the power supply if these all seem to be alright. Ideally you should measure all the output potentials using a multimeter, to check that they are within a few percent of their rated voltages. The test meter does not need to be anything particularly fancy, and a very inexpensive type is adequate for this type of thing. It will also have resistance

ranges that are useful for such things as testing fuses and leads. A simple "multimeter", as they are usually termed, is more than a little useful for anyone involved in DIY PC fault finding.

Note that PC power supplies are of a fairly complex type known as "switching" supplies. These are efficient supplies which permit the relatively high output powers required by a PC to be met by a unit that is of reasonably small dimensions. A practical consequence of the use of a switching power supply is that it will almost certainly shut down completely (probably even cutting off the mains supply to the monitor supply outlet) unless it is connected to a load of some kind. Consequently, when the output voltages are measured the power supply unit must be connected to the motherboard and at least one disk drive.

Replacing a power supply is a fairly straightforward job. With all the leads disconnected and the four retaining screws removed from the rear panel of the computer, it should be possible to remove the faulty unit after a little careful manoeuvring. Provided the replacement is of the correct type, it should slide into place without too much difficulty, and the four fixing screws for the original power supply should fit the new one. Make sure the new supply is of the correct rating (150 watts for a PC or PC XT, 200 watts for an AT, and 220 watts for most 80386 based PCs). Although PC power supplies have been physically well standardised in the past, there are now plenty of clones in non-standard cases, and using physically non-standard power supply units. You therefore need to take a certain amount of care to ensure that a replacement power supply has the correct physical characteristics, as well as the correct power rating.

As much of the power supply's circuitry is connected direct to the mains supply, do not try removing the metal covers and delving around inside. To do so would risk sustaining a very dangerous electric shock, and would be unlikely to effect a repair. Power supply failures usually result in substantial damage to the components, and it is not usually worthwhile attempting repairs anyway.

General

When a PC has been in use for a year or two it will some-times start to produce intermittent faults, such as the odd disk problem, the display failing to operate, or ports not responding properly. This could be due to faults in various parts of the computer, but this type of general and intermittent failure often seems to be the result of bad contacts between the various modules in the system. Modular construction certainly has its advantages, but there is a definite drawback in the form of numerous non-soldered connections all over the system.

If problems of this type should occur, the cure is to take out the expansion cards, disconnect all the cables, give everything a clean with switch or contact cleaner, and then reassemble everything. It is not a bad idea to give the computer this treatment annually anyway, rather than waiting for the occasional error message to be pro-duced before taking any action. Taking out the expansion cards, disconnecting all the hard and floppy disk leads, etc., and then reassembling everything is not exactly a high-tech job. On the other hand, it is very easy to forget which way round leads connect, and things of this nature.

To avoid possible problems when reassembling the computer, it is advisable to make notes and, if necessary, quick sketches before taking it apart. In particularly, if there are two identical connectors, make sure you know where to reconnect each one. If necessary, put identifying marks on cables or connectors so that there is no risk of getting them swopped over later on. Most computer con-nectors are polarised types so that there is no risk of fitting them the wrong way round. However, there may be exceptions and you should make a note of the correct orientation for any non-polarised connectors. You will often find that pin numbers are marked on connectors, making the correct orientation obvious. In some cases you will need quite a powerful magnifier in order to read the numbers, which are often moulded into a plastic part of the connector in minute lettering.

When giving the system a clean of this kind, do not ignore parts such as printer and keyboard leads. Disconnecting these and cleaning both connectors should help to keep the system in good and error-free operation.

Chapter 6

DIY PCs

Due to the modular construction of PCs, and the availability of all the components needed to build one, it is not too difficult to produce your own PC. We are talking here in terms of a simple assembly job, with ready-made boards etc. being slotted and bolted together. Building your own PC from scratch, complete with multi-layer motherboard, is probably not a practical proposition.

If you should decide to build your own PC you need to be aware of the potential advantages and drawbacks. Putting together your own PC is an interesting project which is likely to teach you a great deal about the anatomy and workings of these computers. There are potential money savings to be made, but you need to proceed with caution. It would actually be quite easy to put together a PC that would cost considerably more than a ready made equivalent from one of the larger PC manufacutrers. In order to produce a bargain PC some careful shopping around is called for.

Probably the main attraction is that of being able to put together a machine that precisely meets your requirements. You do not need to buy anything that you do not really need, or that you have already. You can choose whatever monitor and display card you like best, and also the hard disk, style of case, etc. With most ready-made systems this degree of freedom is lacking. You either buy a system of the desired specification and accept whatever display board etc. that particular manufacturer fits, or you buy a fairly low specification computer and upgrade it to meet your requirements (probably discarding a few items supplied as part of the original system in the process).

It is only fair to point out that some manufacturers are more flexible, and will supply computers minus such things as the keyboard, display card, and monitor, if that is what you want. This in a way gives the best of both worlds in that you have a good quality basic system from a respectable manufacturer, probably complete with any support software etc. that is supplied with complete systems. This virtually guarantees that the finished unit will work flawlessly, with no niggling little problems. You can fit onto this basic computer whatever display etc. suits your requirements best, and will waste nothing on unwanted items. The final cost is likely to be somewhat more than a totally DIY PC, but you have what is in many ways a more desirable end-product. The resale value of a computer of this type is likely to be significantly greater than that of a no-name home constructed PC. This is certainly an approach worth pursuing, and one that I would wholeheartedly recommend.

If we now consider the drawbacks of the DIY approach, I suppose that the main one is simply that you have no guarantee of success. Provided the components you use are of reasonable quality, it is unlikely that you would be left with a computer that refused to work at all. Even using components of the "cheap and cheerful" variety it is still highly unlikely that you would be left with an unusable computer. However, there can be minor problems with such things as getting the keyboard to produce all the correct on-screen characters, and switching between normal and "turbo" mode. With a ready-made machine the manufacturer should have sorted out any problems of this type for you. With a DIY PC you might get some assistance from the company that sold you the motherboard or other relevant components, but they might not be willing or able to provide much aid. If you are only buying a few PC components at "knock-down" prices from a company, it is debatable as to whether you could reasonably expect much assistance from them.

As already pointed out, a "no-name" PC, whether of DIY origins or produced by a small and short lived company, will not command the same sort of price on the secondhand market as a "big name" machine. This is not to say that a DIY PC will be unsaleable. At the time of writing this, there seems to be plenty of demand for secondhand PCs, and any PC is likely to fetch a reasonable price. This situation could change, but there seems little likelihood of it doing so in the near future.

It is now quite common for PCs to have a 12 month on-site maintenance agreement included in the purchase price. There is usually the option of extending the agreement by up to four years at a reasonable price. Where on-site maintenance is not included as standard it is almost invariably available as an optional extra. With a DIY PC you might not be able to arrange on-site maintenance, but even if you can, it might be prohibitively expensive. You will get guarantees on the individual components in the system of course, but to a large extent you will be responsible for servicing the computer and bearing the cost of any replacement parts. You might be lucky and have years of trouble-free operation, or you might have to spend large sums of money replacing defunct components that are outside their guarantee period. This is a risk you will probably have to accept if you take the DIY approach.

If you should decide to try your hand at PC assembly, much of the information you will need has been provided in the previous chapters. Taking a hard disk as an example, it does not make much difference whether you are fitting one to a PC as an upgrade, or as a component in a DIY PC. Either way it will need to be physically mounted in the case, formatted, etc., in exactly the same way. Therefore, in this discussion of DIY PCs we will not cover all aspects in great detail, as this would to a large extent be repeating information provided in earlier chapters. We will consider matters in fairly broad terms, and reference to the appropriate chapter should be made if you require more detailed information on a particular topic.

Motherboard, Memory and Cases
Basically a PC consists of the following components:

Motherboard
Memory
Floppy Disk Drive
Floppy Disk Controller Card
Hard Disk Drive
Hard Disk Controller
Power Supply Unit
Ports
Display Card
Monitor
Keyboard
Cables, bolts, etc.
MS/DOS Operating System

We will consider each of these in turn, starting with the motherboard.

It is essential to choose the motherboard first, since several of the other components must be selected to suit the particular motherboard selected. The motherboard determines what type of computer the finished product will be (XT, AT, 80386 AT, or 80386SX AT). An XT board will provide the cheapest finished product, should be reasonably easy to deal with, but even if a fast "turbo" board is used, the finished computer will lack computing power by modern standards. Obviously an XT compatible is perfectly suitable for many requirements, but it does not provide good "future proofing". An 80286 based turbo AT motherboard is quite a good choice as it is unlikely to give any real problems when building and setting up the computer, it is reasonably powerful, and will probably be able to run any PC software you will wish to use with the computer. The difference in cost between an XT and an AT computer is relatively low these days, making the AT an attractive proposition.

An 80386SX is an increasingly popular choice of microprocessor for both ready-made and DIY PCs. You have what is basically a standard AT computer, but one which is capable of running 80386 software should this ever become necessary. It is a bit more expensive than an equivalent 80286 computer, and in the main will not give better performance than one of the faster 80286 based ATs. An 80386SX board virtually guarantees compatibility with any PC software now, and during the next few years. While 80386 based AT motherboards offer the greatest power and should run any PC software well, they are perhaps a little risky in that they offer the greatest scope for problems. The faster 80386 motherboards in particular, have gained something of a reputation for being a bit temperamental and fussy about the expansion cards they will operate with. This reputation may not be fully justified, but with the relatively high cost of 80386 based motherboards you need to proceed with due caution if you decide to base a DIY PC on one of these. When purchasing any motherboard you need to ensure that any software utilities which are needed to make the board fully operational are supplied with the board, but this is especially important with the more sophisticated motherboards.

When obtaining a motherboard make sure that it is supplied complete with suitable BIOS chips. These can be bought separately, but it is generally better if you can obtain a BIOS ready fitted that is fully compatible with the motherboard. If you fit any "off the shelf" BIOS chips there is a risk that the system may not operate entirely satisfactorily. In particular, "turbo" mode switching via the keyboard has a habit of not functioning properly unless a correctly matched BIOS is fitted. Any good BIOS should enable the computer to function properly as far as basic IBM compatibility is concerned, but if you buy an "off the shelf" BIOS, remember that PC XT and AT types are totally different. Also bear in mind that the two BIOS chips for an AT are not the same, and must be fitted in the right sockets. No damage should result if they are inadvertently swopped over, and so you can always adopt trial and error here if necessary. These days virtually all motherboards, whether of the XT or AT variety, seem to be supplied with a properly matched BIOS chip set. If you are building an AT type computer

I would strongly recommend the use of a motherboard having a BIOS that incorporates a setup program for the clock/calendar and CMOS RAM. If you do not have diagnostics software and hard disk formatting/testing software, a BIOS that incorporates these programs is more than a little helpful.

An XT motherboard will, of course, have configuration switches that must be set up to suit the amount of memory fitted, etc. It also seems to be quite normal for AT motherboards to have a number of configuration switches or (more commonly) a number of jumper blocks. These set up the motherboard to suit the particular type of memory chips you are using, the default clock speed, and things of this nature. These tend to vary considerably from one computer to another, and it is a matter of carefully going through the manual and making any con-figuration adjustments before fitting the motherboard into the case.

Most motherboards, regardless of the microprocessor they utilize, are XT size these days. 80286, 80386, and 80386SX based boards almost invariably seem to have both XT and AT board mounting holes, so that they can fit into XT or AT style cases. Note though, that there are a few AT type motherboards that will only fit AT cases. The standard XT case is a type which has a so-called flip-up lid. This is a hinged lid which can be raised at the front once release buttons on opposite sides of the case have been pressed. One or two struts then hold the lid open so that you can work on the interior of the unit. A standard AT type case is a bit larger and has an outer casing (top, front, and sides) that is completely removed by undoing five screws on the rear panel, and then pulling the outer casing forwards and clear of the chassis.

In recent times there seems to have a proliferation of alternative PC case styles. These are mostly of the "tower", "mini tower", or some form of "slimline" variety. You need to be a bit wary of some of these alter-native case styles, as you might find it difficult to fit everything in place. For DIY purposes there is a lot to be said for standard XT and AT cases, simply because they are reasonably well standardised. There are plenty of "off the shelf" power supplies, motherboards, etc. that will fit them with no difficulty. Also, their relatively large size means that there is plenty of space inside, making it easy to fit everything in, and leaving plenty of room for lots of full length expansion cards if necessary.

If available space for the finished computer is going to be a problem, you might find that a conventional XT or AT case fitted vertically on the floor in an inexpensive stand is a good way of tackling the problem. It is a method I have found to work well in practice. Alternatively, a full-size tower case can be used. These provide plenty of room for expansion, are mostly very impressive visually, and are generally highly desirable. Probably their only major drawback is that they mostly seem to be quite expensive. A standard AT or XT type case fitted in a floor stand is a less neat solution, but what is likely to be a much more affordable one. If you do opt for any form of non-standard case, do check that it will take the size of motherboard you intend to use.

When buying a case you should be careful to obtain one that is described as "with kit", or something along these lines. One of the problems when building your own PC is that a lot of small items of hardware are required, such as disk mounting rails for an AT, mounting pillars and screws for the motherboard, etc. Some of the screws are probably general items that can be obtained from hardware stores, electronic component retailers, and other sources. Much of this hardware is not the type of thing that is easy to obtain though, and in some cases a specialist PC component supplier is the only likely source. Buying a case that is supplied complete with all the necessary hardware can save a great deal of hassle, and is likely to be cheaper than buying a cheap case that is not supplied with any hardware, and then buying all the necessary odds and ends separately.

In the past it has been normal for motherboards to be

designed to take memory in the form of DRAM chips such as 4164s, 41256s, and 41000s. Virtually all XT boards still seem to be designed to take RAM in this form, but with the various AT class computers there has been a strong trend in favour of SIMMs. Some AT motherboards seem able to take DRAM chips, SIMMs, or a combination of the two. There is a new development in the form of plug-in cards which take the memory chips or SIMMs. These often take up the space that would normally be occupied by a standard expansion slot, but the slot for the memory card is not in the form of a normal expansion type. It is a special type, which in the case of an 80386 based motherboard will be a 32 bit slot. This obviously requires a special memory board which should be bought with the motherboard. You may have a choice of two or three memory boards, offering different maximum capacities.

The manual supplied with the motherboard should make it clear what type of SIMM or DRAM chips are needed, including the minimum acceptable speed rating. In fact it is probably best to check with the motherboard supplier prior to purchase that the amount of memory you require can be fitted onto the board. Motherboards are mainly designed to be quite flexible with regard to memory types and capacities. However, you may find that the particular capacity you require is not supported by the board, and that some larger amount must be fitted. For example, you might require an AT motherboard with 1.5 megabytes of RAM, but the board might only be able to accommodate 1 megabyte of 41256 DRAMs, or 2/4 megabytes of 41000 DRAMs. You could opt for 1 megabyte on the motherboard plus 512k on a memory expansion card, but simply fitting 2 megabytes on the motherboard is likely to be a better prospect. The difference in cost would probably be minimal, and with all the RAM on the motherboard it will run faster. The extra 512k of RAM would probably prove to be quite useful. Most suppliers will sell motherboards ready fitted with a specified amount of memory, but it is often cheaper to

142

buy the bare motherboard, obtain the memory from a specialist supplier, and then fit the DRAMs and (or) SIMMs yourself.

Power Supplies

The standard these days seems to be a 150 watt power supply for XT compatible computers, and a 200 watt type for AT compatible types. 80386 based PCs usually have a slightly larger power supply, with about 220 or 230 watts being typical. With modern motherboards, expansion cards, disk drives, etc. tending to use less power than those of a few years ago, there is a temptation to cut costs by opting for a fairly small power supply when building an AT type machine. In most cases this is probably quite safe, but it is not a course of action I would recommend. The difference in cost between a supply having a rating of 150 watts and one having a rating of 200 watts or more is not usually particularly great. By opting for a smaller supply unit you are risking problems unless you are sure that the computer is built from suitable low power components. Probably the main drawback is that many PCs seem to end up with large amounts of memory and expansion cards these days. By using a small power supply you might be compromising what might be termed the "upgradability" of the computer.

Provided you use a standard case there should be no difficulty in finding a suitable power supply to fit it. If you obtain one of the non-standard types it may well be sold together with the power supply as a package deal, or your supplier will probably have a matching power supply unit on offer. If the case is in any way non-standard, make quite sure that the power supply you obtain is compatible. With any non-standard case it is probably best to obtain the case and power supply from the same source, with an assurance that they are fully compatible.

Make sure that you get the two power supply connectors for the motherboard fitted the right way round. They are identical, and can easily be accidentally swopped over. Surprisingly perhaps, getting them swopped over will not necessarily result in any damage to the motherboard. Safety circuits within the power supply might detect the problem and prevent the supply from operating. It is best not to risk it though. The leads from the power supply invariably seem to have wires of different colours for the various output voltages. One of the leads for the motherboard will have three leads of the same colour (the +5 volt supplies). This fits onto the connector nearest the front of the computer — the other lead fits onto the connector nearest the rear of the computer. These are "PL9" and "PL8" on the original AT board and some clones, but not all clones use this method of numbering.

Disk Drives

The inclusion of at least one floppy disk drive is mandatory with a PC, and there is a lot to be said in favour of twin drives even if the computer is also to be equipped with a hard disk drive. The choice is between 3.5 inch or 5.25 inch floppy drives. The 720k 3.5 inch type and 360k 5.25 inch type are the ones used on PC and PC XT computers. The equivalents for AT style machines are the high density 1.44 megabyte and 1.2 megabyte types respectively. The lower density drives are suitable for second drives on AT computers, and the 360k is popular in this role, as it gives total compatibility with XT 360k disk drives. However, do not obtain a drive of this type unless you are sure that the BIOS supports it.

3.5 inch drives are now the industry standard, and presumably the 5.25 inch varieties will disappear in the fullness of time. However, at the present time the 5.25 inch formats still seem to be more widely supported than the 3.5 inch type. This is perhaps not surprising when you consider the large number of PCs fitted with 5.25 inch drives that have been sold over the past few years. In fact a fair proportion of the PCs currently being sold seem to be equipped with only 5.25 inch drives. Which size of disk drive represents the best choice depends on the individual circumstances. If you already have equipment that uses 5.25 inch disks, but none that uses 3.5 inch types, you will probably have little choice to opt for a 5.25 inch drive in order to maintain compatibility with existing equipment and software. A 3.5 inch drive is then probably only viable as a second drive, and is a very desirable asset. If you are starting from scratch, or you already have equipment that is fitted with a 3.5 inch drive or drives, a 3.5 inch drive then probably represents the best option. Virtually all current PC software is available on 3.5 inch disks, and the lack of a 5.25 inch drive will probably only be a minor hardship.

The choice of hard disk is obviously dependent on the level of performance and capacity required. For many purposes the ever popular (and cheap) 20 megabyte units with an access time of 65 milliseconds will suffice. If the computer will be mainly used with disk intensive software, such as some CAD and database programs, then a faster access drive will be desirable. If large amounts of data must be stored, or the computer will be used with several programs, a higher capacity drive is also desirable. Although at one time most PC software was supplied on one 360k disk, these days many programs seem to be supplied on ten or more of these disks. Even given that it is not usually necessary for all the information on every disk to be transferred to the hard disk during the installation process, many programs now seem to require a fair amount of disk space even before you start to generate any data. Some three to four megabytes would be by no means untypical.

For most purposes a hard disk having a capacity of 40 megabytes or so, and an access time of 40 milliseconds will suffice. If the computer will be used with software that uses lots of program overlays it might be better to opt for a slightly faster type, such as a 20 or 28 millisecond type. Hard disks having this sort of capacity and access times are widely available, and due to their popularity are surprisingly inexpensive. Higher capacity disks, which almost invariably offer fast access times as well, are certainly very desirable, but are often quite expensive. You need to be quite sure that the extra capacity and performance is really needed before paying out large sums of money for a high capacity hard disk drive.

Connecting cables etc. for floppy and hard disk drives, plus differences between XT and AT hard disk controllers and installation was covered in Chapter 3. Consequently we will not cover the same ground again here. Obviously you will need a floppy disk controller, and these are all 8 bit types, most of which are suitable for use in PC, PC XT, and AT computers. However, a few types do not support high density drives, and are strictly for PC and PC XT use. Any modern controller card capable of operating with high density drives should support both the 5.25 inch and 3.5 inch varieties. I think I am right in stating that any PC floppy disk controller will support both 360k and 720k floppy drives. With AT style computers it is normal to use a combined hard/floppy disk controller. These will control two hard disk drives and two floppy disk drives. Using a controller of this type has the advantage of only occupying a single expansion slot (albeit a 16 bit full length type), and is likely to prove cheaper than using separate controllers.

For XT computers both separate and combined floppy/hard disk controllers are in common use. If you are fitting a hard disk drive at the outset, a combined type is likely to be the best option. It will only occupy one expansion slot, which will probably not even need to be a full length type. It is also likely to be cheaper than buying separate controller cards. If the computer is only going to have a floppy drive or drives, a multi-function card might be the best choice. Some of these seem to provide an amazing array of functions, including such combinations as parallel port, floppy disk controller, serial port, clock/calendar and joystick port. They are often very much cheaper than two or three cards to provide the same functions, and have the added advantage of leaving plenty of expansion slots free.

Ports, Displays and Keyboards
You may well find that all the ports you require are

provided as extras on such things as the display card and (or) a multi-function card providing the floppy controller and the clock/calendar. There are plenty of expansion cards which will provide parallel and serial ports if necessary, and these are 8 bit cards which are suitable for PC, PC XT, or AT style computers. To be entirely accurate, the serial cards for XT computers are based on a different chip to those for AT computers. The PC and PC XT computers should have a serial port based on a chip in the 8250 series, while AT serial ports should utilize the 16450. In practice a lot of AT clones seem to be sold complete with 8250 based serial port cards, and some PC expansion card retailers seem to sell cards of this type for use in any type of PC, including ATs. In practice this does not normally matter, since MS/DOS seems to be able to cope with either type of port. Apparently, some other operating systems are less accommodating though, and could give problems unless the correct type of card is used in an AT.

It is perhaps worth mentioning joystick ports here. As the PC was for many years used almost solely as a business computer in the U.K., joystick ports and suitable joysticks were at one time very difficult to obtain. Now the PC is widely used in a wide range of applications, including a large number that are at least occasionally used for playing computer games. Joysticks for the PC and joystick ports are now widely available, and are quite inexpensive. These are the same for PC, PC XT, and AT computers, and are something that is unlikely to give any problems. Note that PC joysticks are of the potentiometer type, and not the switch type that are used with most other types of computer (notably the popular Commodore and Atari machines). Consequently, they are totally incompatible with these joysticks, and changing their 9 pin D connectors for 15 pin D types (as used on PC games ports) will not permit them to be used with a PC.

There is little I can add about display adaptors and monitors, as this subject was covered fairly comprehensively in Chapter 4. You pay your money and take your choice from the wide range of display types on offer. An advantage of the DIY approach is that you can choose the particular makes of display card and monitor that you prefer, rather than being tied to whatever make the computer manufacturer happens to supply.

Your basic choice of keyboard is between the old 84 key types and the more recent 102 key type. The latter is the type that most people prefer, but in my experience there can be difficulties when trying to use one of these. The hardware and operating system are designed primarily for use with U.S. keyboards, and a U.K. type might in the case of a few keys produce incorrect on-screen characters. With 84 key types any problems of this type are generally quite small, and may well be fully sorted out by a suitable entry in the CONFIG.SYS file to let the system know that the U.K. character set must be used. The problem is often more severe with the 102 key types, where several keys are effectively swopped over, and the "\" key often has no effect at all. A keyboard redefinition program then seems to be the only solution, but note that with some BIOSs you may find that the "\" key is still inoperative. If the BIOS does not recognise it, there may be no alternatives to getting by without this key, or fitting a different BIOS!

The keyboards for XT and AT type computers have the same type of connector, but they use a slightly different method of interfacing to the main unit. Virtually all the PC keyboards currently on offer seem to be switchable to operate with either type of computer, and a few automatically switch to suit the computer to which they are connected. Prices for keyboards vary enormously. So does their build quality, and in general you get what you pay for. For many purposes an inexpensive keyboard will suffice, but if you do a lot of typing, and (or) can type quite fast, a good quality type will probably prove to be well worth the extra expenditure.

Beating the System
The operating system for a home constructed computer represents something of a problem. Presumably the vast

majority of users will wish to use MS/DOS, but Microsoft only permit this to be sold together with a computer by a licensed manufacturer who has checked that it works satisfactorily with the computer in question. On the face of it, there is no legal way of obtaining the MS/DOS operating system for a home assembled PC. If you already have MS/DOS for another PC it will almost certainly provide trouble-free operation on your home constructed computer. Unfortunately, it is probably a breach of copyright, and illegal if you use a single copy of the operating system on two computers.

In practice it does seem to be possible to obtain MS/DOS from a few software retailers. Presumably someone somewhere is breaking an agreement if this software is sold on its own, and not with a computer. However, I think that I am correct in saying that if you buy a genuine copy of MS/DOS (not a "pirated" copy), you are perfectly entitled to use it and are not breaking any laws in doing so. Although MS/DOS has now moved on to version 4.01 (and possibly beyond by the time you read this), version 3.3 is still available at a somewhat lower cost, and should satisfy most requirements. It is the version that I still use.

There is an alternative to MS/DOS in the form of DR/DOS from Digital Research. This is available as an "off the shelf" operating system, and the latest versions seem to offer excellent DOS compatibility, plus an impressive range of features. For the DIY PC builder this operating system perhaps represents the best (and possibly only) fully legitimate solution to the problem.

Getting It Together

Once you have all the components, actually putting everything together is usually fairly easy. There may be one or two slightly awkward bits to deal with, and the main difficulties are at the places in the case where there is little spare room. The gap between the rear of the disk drives and the front of the power supply can often be quite small, making it difficult to fit the connectors onto the drive. There should be just sufficient space to permit this, but you can always partially remove the drives in order to permit the connectors to be fitted if things are really tight. This is certainly preferable to forcing things and risking damage to the drives and connectors.

The general layout for a PC, whether of the XT or AT varieties, is shown in Figure 6.1. This assumes that a

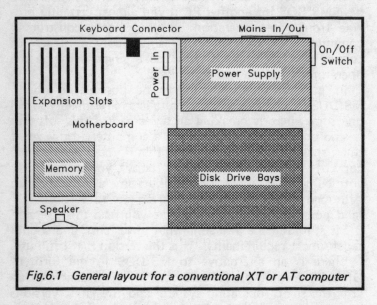

Fig.6.1 General layout for a conventional XT or AT computer

standard case is used, and the layout is totally different for some non-standard types. With one of these cases it will probably be fairly obvious where everything fits, but if in doubt you can always consult the supplier, or an explanatory leaflet might be supplied with the case. The power supply is bolted to the rear panel of the case, usually via four bolts which pass through ready drilled holes in the case and into threaded holes in the rear panel of the power supply unit. Incidentally, all the PC cases I have encountered have had all the holes and cut-outs already made, but you may need to do a small amount of filing in order to get everything to fit correctly. The power supply has a built-in on/off switch which fits into the cut-out at the rear of the case's right hand side panel.

It seems to be standard for PC power supplies to have a "Euro-connector" for the mains supply input, and plugs/leads to match up with these are readily available. The plug on a replacement electric kettle lead is marginally different, but a lead of this type will do if you can not obtain the correct type. Apart from the mains inlet (the plug), most PC power supplies also have a mains outlet (the socket next to the inlet plug). This is intended to be used as the power source for the monitor. It is a switched outlet, and if the monitor is powered from this and left in the "on" state, it will be switched on and off in sympathy with the computer. You do not have to power the monitor from this outlet of course, but it is a neat and convenient way of handling things. Suitable connectors can be obtained from the large electronic retailers, and probably from most electrical retailers as well.

Disk drive mounting has already been covered, and will not be dealt with again here. Mounting the motherboard is different for XT and AT types. An XT style motherboard has nine mounting holes arranged in three rows of three. However, note that some modern XT boards are less than full size, and that they consequently lack the front row of three holes. XT motherboards are normally mounted using metal pillars using the arrangement shown in Figure 6.2(a). The exact method of mounting AT style boards seems to vary somewhat from one case to another, but they are usually fixed by a combination of plastic mounting pillars (Figure 6.2(b)) and screws which pass through holes in the board and into threaded mounting pillars moulded into the case. When fitting any motherboard into the case, make sure that none of the fixings are overlooked and omitted. When expansion cards are placed into their slots it is often necessary to use a fair amount of pressure in order to persuade them to slide into place. If any of the mountings for the motherboard are omitted, there is a slight risk that this will result in the board flexing, and possibly becoming damaged in the process.

151

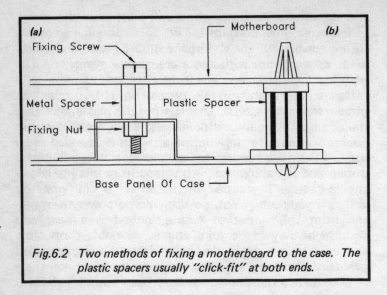

Motherboard

Fixing Screw

Metal Spacer → Plastic Spacer →

Fixing Nut →

Base Panel Of Case →

Fig.6.2 Two methods of fixing a motherboard to the case. The plastic spacers usually "click-fit" at both ends.

It is generally easier to fit DRAM chips before the motherboard is fixed inside the case. SIMMs can often be added quite easily once the board has been fixed in place. Any configuration switches or jumper leads are more easily adjusted before the motherboard is mounted in the case.

With the main components in place it is then just a matter of adding the expansion cards and wiring everything up. If the computer is a type having a hard disk, initially it is advisable to leave the hard disk disconnected, and get the computer up and running as a floppy type first. When it is working properly, then proceed to connect the hard disk, do a low level format, etc. Remember that with an AT computer you will need to run the setup program in order to set the time/date, and the correct configuration information. If you do not have a suitable setup program, it is important to obtain a motherboard which has a BIOS with a built-in setup program. Without placing the right configuration information in the CMOS RAM the computer is almost certain to only operate in a very limited form, probably ignoring some of the disk drives and memory. You will also be unable to set the clock/calendar correctly.

This problem does not arise with XT style computers, where configuration switches are used to set everything up correctly. If you have a clock/calendar card in an XT computer, this will only be of any use if it is supplied with utility programs to enable the time and date to be set, and to integrate it with the operating system. Without this software you will be unable to set the time and date, and MS/DOS will simply ignore the unit anyway. Always check that the necessary utility software is included before buying a card of this type.

Building your own PC is a very interesting and rewarding project, and one that I would certainly recommend. On the other hand, it is probably something that you should only undertake if you like a bit of a challenge, as there are likely to be minor problems to negotiate, such as getting all the necessary leads and odd bits of hardware, getting the keyboard properly redefined, etc. Provided you can take minor problems in your stride, producing a working PC should not be too difficult. If not, it is probably best to stick to ready-made units from established manufacturers.

If you do a lot of PC upgrading, you could well end up with a lot of "left overs" such as an old display card, monitor, perhaps even a 20 megabyte hard disk drive left over after upgrading to a larger, faster type. I put together an XT compatible having quite a respectable specification using "left overs", secondhand memory chips, bits and pieces bought cheap from friends, and even one or two new components such as the case and power supply! Putting together a computer in this fashion can produce a very inexpensive but very useful stand-by PC.

Chapter 7

DEVELOPMENTS

Since this book was written there have been developments in PC specifications. Some aspects of PC computing have not actually changed that much. For example, today's V.G.A. and super V.G.A. displays are much the same as those of a few years ago. There are no real signs of any superior form of display replacing these and becoming a new standard. On the other hand, there have been big developments in other departments.

Processors
Probably the biggest changes are in the types of microprocessor used in current PCs. The 8088 and 8086 would seem to be totally obsolete now, and are probably not used in any PCs currently being produced. The 80286 microprocessor also seems to be obsolete, including all "turbo" versions having clock speeds of 10MHz or more. Some of the more powerful 80*** series microprocessors have fallen to such low prices that the 8088, 8086, and 80286 were squeezed out at the bottom end of the market. Using a less powerful processor only saved a couple of percent on the total price of a basic PC system, but gave (typically) a 50% reduction in performance. Even if someone did not need the extra power of an 80386SX microprocessor right away, it made sense to spend a few pounds more to buy one as it gave better "future-proofing".

There still seems to be a fair selection of 8088, 8086, and 80286 based PCs on sale, and at very low prices in most cases. However, although these may look like tempting bargains, bear in mind that there is more and more software coming along which these computers can not run at all, or will only run in a limited fashion. In particular, to run most Windows software well requires at least an 80386SX processor, and preferably something a bit more

155

advanced than this. The low prices of PCs based on old microprocessors reflects their relative power and usefulness.

The range of microprocessors currently based in PCs is a bit bewildering. It is complicated by the fact that there are now several companies producing 80*** series microprocessors. Many of these chips are designed to operate at different clock frequencies to the standard Intel devices. The basic PC in most ranges these days is one based on a 80386SX running at about 25MHz. Even these now seem to be dying out, and something like a 33MHz 80386DX or a 25MHz 80486SX based machine is rapidly becoming the "bottom end" PC.

The 80486SX differs from the 80486DX in that it does not have the maths co-processor built-in, but this can be added later. This is just a matter of adding a 80487 chip, much like upgrading and 80386DX using an 80387 maths co-processor. In terms of overall speed there is not much to choose between an 80486SX running at 25MHz, and an 80386DX operating at about 33 to 40MHz. However, there is a potential advantage in buying a 80486SX based computer in that most of these can take an "Overdrive" upgrade. This uses so-called clock doubling techniques to provide a substantial boost in performance.

An "Overdrive" upgrade can take three basic forms, one of which can really only be undertaken at a properly equipped service centre. Most 80486SX based PCs can use one of the other methods, which are easily undertaken by users. One method involves the replacement of the original microprocessor with the new "Overdrive" chip. The other method simply involves adding a new microprocessor into the upgrade socket on the motherboard, much like adding a maths co-processor. The old processor must be switched off, but this is usually done automatically by a microswitch. The replacement method is the only one that is applicable if a motherboard lacks the upgrade socket. Many of the early 80486SX motherboards do not have the "Overdrive" upgrade socket, but it is included on practically all motherboards produced recently. It is obviously best to make use of the upgrade socket where possible.

In theory the "Overdrive" upgrade effectively doubles the system clock frequency from 25MHz to 50MHz. However, speed tests on PCs generally show an increase in performance of around 70% rather than the theoretical 100% improvement. This still represents a substantial improvement in performance though, giving a 80486 machine with an effective clock speed of about 42MHz. An upgraded 25MHz 80486SX PC therefore has a level of performance which lies somewhere between 33MHz and 50MHz 80486DX based PCs.

Upgrading tends to be a relatively expensive method of obtaining high performance though, and it is generally better to buy a more powerful computer from the start whenever possible. Although 33MHz 80486DX based PCs were very expensive at one time, they are now quite affordable. This processor currently represents the best option for someone who requires a powerful PC without spending large sums of money. The cost of PCs using 50MHz and 66MHz 80486DX microprocessors has also fallen a great deal recently, but these remain relatively expensive.

The latest Intel microprocessor in the 80*** series does not actually have a type number. It has apparently been given a name rather than a type number because it is possible to own the copyright in a name, but not in a type number. It is called the "Pentium", and it is a very powerful microprocessor. Although it is not officially known as the 80586, this is effectively what it is. The "Pentium" normally operates at a clock frequency of 60MHz or 66MHz, but when running ordinary PC software it is nearly twice as efficient as a 80486DX running at the same clock frequency. In other words, a "Pentium" running at 66MHz is roughly equivalent to a hypothetical 80486DX running at around 115 to 120MHz. A "Pentium" powered PC is clearly a very desirable piece of equipment, but at the present time the cost of "Pentium" PCs is very high.

Hard Disks

Hard disks represent another aspect of computing in which there have been some large changes in recent years. A 40 megabyte hard drive was considered perfectly adequate for most purposes until not so long ago. These days 40 megabytes accommodates little more than DOS, Windows, and one of the more advanced Windows word processors. About 90 megabytes is a more realistic minimum these days, and many PC users now regard double that as a more satisfactory amount of storage space. Fortunately, hard disk drives having capacities of around 150 to 200 megabytes cost rather less than a 40 megabyte drive did a few years ago.

The biggest change in PC hard disks is the sudden demise of MFM and RLL drives and controllers. IDE drives now dominate the PC hard disk market. I have seen various explanations of this acronym, but "integrated disk electronics" (or something similar) seems to be the most popular choice. An IDE drive does not require a controller card in the conventional sense. An IDE controller card, like an MFM type, usually includes the floppy disk controller as well. However, that is the only electronics that it contains. The hard disk controller section simply provides a method of connection from the drive to the buses of the motherboard.

The connections from the controller to the hard drive are carried via a ribbon cable fitted with IDC connectors, much like an MFM hard disk drive cable. The cable is a 40-way type terminated in a 2 × 20-way IDC connector at each end (not an edge connector at the drive end of the cable). A twin drive cable connects straight through to both drives with no twists in the cable. Links or switches on each drive configure it to operate as the sole drive, drive 1 in a two drive system, or drive 2 in a twin drive system. Every drive should be supplied with a small booklet which includes this type of configuration information.

No hard disk controller is needed with an IDE drive simply because the controller is built into the disk drive. There is a big advantage in this system in that the controller should always be a perfect match for the drive, and the drive should therefore always give optimum performance. Physically installing an IDE drive is much the same as installing an MFM type, but having the controller and drive as one unit results in some important differences in the setting up and formatting procedure. It should perhaps be pointed out that normal IDE hard disk drives are not suitable for use in XT style PCs as they require a 16 bit (AT type) expansion bus. They should work properly with any PC which has at least an 80286 microprocessor.

In normal AT hard disk fashion, the first job after physically installing the drive is to use the setup program to enter details of the drive into the CMOS RAM. IDE hard disk drives are very flexible in this respect, and they can mimic practically any hard disk drive in the list of supported drives. The obvious proviso is that you must not choose a drive type which has a higher capacity than the IDE drive you are using. In other words, a 124 megabyte hard disk drive can "pretend" to be virtually any drive having a capacity of 124 megabytes or less, but could not be used safely with the computer setup for a 150 megabyte type.

If you are upgrading an old PC you will probably have no choice but to change over to an IDE hard drive, since MFM and RLL types are now unobtainable, apart from a few surplus units that might still be in circulation. A new controller card will therefore be needed, together with a new hard disk cable. Fortunately, an IDE hard/floppy disk controller card and a hard disk cable do not cost a great deal these days. In the setup program you will have to choose the hard disk type that makes best use of your drive's capabilities. If you are putting together a new computer, or upgrading a recent one, the setup program should enable you to fully utilize the hard drive's capacity. With a modern BIOS it is possible to specify the number of heads, sectors, and cylinders for your hard drive. This information is then stored in the extended CMOS RAM, together with the time, date, and other standard setup information.

One might reasonably expect that the hard drive specification entered into the setup program would be the actual number of cylinders, sectors, and heads that the drive physically possesses. In practice this is not usually the case when using an IDE drive. If you look-up the physical specification for an IDE drive in its instruction manual, you will almost certainly discover that there are three figures given for the number of sectors per cylinder! The reason for this is that the tracks (cylinders) around the outer part of each disk are longer than those near the middle. In order to make optimum use of the disk's surface area more sectors are used in the outer tracks than in the shorter tracks near the middle of the disk. Typically there would be something like 42 sectors in the longest tracks, 32 in the shortest ones, and 36 sectors in each of the intermediate tracks.

It is not possible to specify more than one figure for the sectors per cylinder parameter when using the setup program. Due to an IDE drive's translating capabilities this does not matter. You can simply use any numbers that make good use of the disk drive's capacity. Practical experience would suggest that it is advisable to use a number for the sectors parameter that is less than the minimum number of physical sectors, or more than the maximum number of physical sectors. In the example given previously, the number of sectors would therefore be given as a value which is less than 32, or more than 42. Using a value in the range 32 to 42 could give problems, as the drive would have to be translating upwards on some cylinders, and downwards on others. This is fine in theory, but some drives seem to have boot-up problems when used in this way. The instruction manual may well include tried and tested values for use in the setup program. These should avoid any boot-up or other reliability problems, as well as utilizing all the drive's available storage space.

Formatting

Another important difference between MFM/RLL and IDE drives is that MFM and RLL drives are supplied totally unformatted, but IDE types have the low level formatting done at the factory. Therefore, no attempt should be made to low level format an IDE drive. This can only be done using a special formatting program, and it is something that the user would not normally need to undertake. It is unlikely that any damage will result if you should accidentally try to low level format an IDE drive using an ordinary low level formatting program. The program may actually proceed normally, and it might appear as though the formatting is being carried out. However, it is unlikely that the drive would actually be doing any formatting. It is best not to try it though, since it is just possible that the disk's formatting would be rearranged slightly, rendering it unusable until proper reformatting had been carried out.

Of course, with the low level formatting being carried out at the factory, there is no need for the user to worry about interleave factors. The optimum interleave factor should be set at the factory.

With no low level formatting being needed, once the setup program has been given the correct information it is just a matter of booting up from a floppy disk. Then the FDISK and FORMAT programs are run, just as for an MFM or RLL hard disk drive.

Floppy Drives

There have been several attempts at producing floppy disk drives that can handle higher capacities than the 1.4 megabytes of a standard high density 3.5 inch floppy drive. These may have been successful technically, but as yet there is no generally accepted standard for floppy disks having capacities beyond 1.4 megabytes. The relatively high cost of the disks for higher capacity drives seems to be a major obstacle to their general acceptance, as do worries about the reliability of the very high capacity disks and drives.

With many PCs now having about four to eight mega-bytes of memory, and some of the larger software packages now running to about 20 megabytes of program code and supporting data, the 1.4 megabyte capacity of a standard 3.5 inch high density drive has become inadequate. There is definitely a need for higher capacity drives. However, it is impossible to recommend any form of very high capacity drive until one or other of the formats becomes established as a true standard.

CD ROMs

CD ROM drives are fast becoming an essential part of a PC system. CD ROMs are starting to be used as a means of distributing large programs, as well as being the standard format for multi-media software of various types. The CDs themselves look just like ordinary 5 inch audio CDs, and are in fact basically the same as ordinary audio CDs. Their maximum capacity is enormous, and over 600 mega-bytes can be stored on a single CD. Using data compression techniques it is actually possible to squeeze well over 1000 megabytes onto one CD. This amount of storage capacity opens up all sorts of possibilities. One CD ROM in my small collection is a complete PD/shareware library on a single CD. If you buy this library in the form of floppy disks you need to have storage space for about 2400 disks!

The CD ROM player can be either an internal unit or an external device. An internal CD ROM drive fits into a bay intended for a 5.25 inch floppy disk drive. A bay intended for a 5.25 inch hard disk drive is clearly unsuitable, since it is necessary to have access to the drive so that the CD can be changed. A controller card and connecting cable are required, and it is advisable to buy the ROM drive, controller card, and connecting cable as a matched kit of parts. This should avoid the possibility of any incompatibility problems.

The setup is basically the same for an external CD ROM drive, but with the drive mounted in its own case, and connected to the back of the computer via a short cable.

Many external units seem to have their own mains power supply units rather than being powered from the computer. An external drive is in many ways the more convenient option. The host PC is likely to be equipped with two floppy drives and a hard disk drive already, which can make it difficult to arrange a suitable bay for the ROM drive. On the other hand, external drives seem to be substantially more expensive than internal units, which makes it worth the effort of finding the space for an internal unit.

In order to be of any practical use a CD ROM drive must have a suitable driver program loaded during boot-up. The driver program is usually in the form of a SYS file which is called up by CONFIG.SYS during the boot-up process. Once the driver program is installed correctly, the CD ROM drive effectively becomes just another disk drive (i.e. drive D: in a twin floppy and single hard drive system). It can be used just like an ordinary hard or floppy drive, except that it is only possible to read from a CD ROM. Due to the high capacities of CD ROMs it is helpful to have some software which makes it easy to find what you want, and then copy it to floppy disk (or whatever). Many CD ROM upgrade kits include a useful utility program of this type.

In the early days of CD ROMs there were no end of incompatibility problems. Things are much more standardised these days, and any modern CD ROM should work properly in any PC ROM drive. Of course, some CD software is machine specific, and you can only use PC compatible software in a PC. However, this is no different to the situation with floppy drives and normal PC software. Some CD ROM software is just masses of text, or other data of a universal nature such as photo CD. This type of software will usually run on a wide range hardware, including modern PC based systems.

Index